CAN MEN AND WOMEN BE *Just* FRIENDS?

Books by Andy Bustanoby

But I Didn't Want a Divorce
Single Parenting
Tough Parenting for Dangerous Times (with Verne Becker)
When Your Mate Is Not a Christian

CAN MEN AND WOMEN BE Just FRIENDS?

ANDY BUSTANOBY

ZondervanPublishingHouse
Grand Rapids, Michigan

A Division of HarperCollinsPublishers

Can Men and Women Be Just Friends?
Copyright © 1985, 1993 by Andy Bustanoby

Requests for information should be addressed to:
Zondervan Publishing House
Grand Rapids, Michigan 49530

Library of Congress Cataloging-in-Publication Data

Bustanoby, André.
    Can men and women be just friends? / Andy Bustanoby. —Rev.
    p. cm.
    ISBN 0-310-58891-X (pbk.)
    1. Interpersonal relations. 2. Friendship. 3. Intimacy.
(Psychology) 4. Man-woman relationships. I. Title.
HM132.B87   1993
302.3'4—dc20   93–11392
                                                  CIP

Unless otherwise indicated, the Scripture text used is the New American Standard Bible, copyright © 1960, 1962, 1963, 1968, 1971, 1972 by the Lockman Foundation, La Habra, California.

Edited by Carol Uridil, James E. Ruark, Lori J. Walburg, and Jan Ortiz
Designed by Ann Cherryman and James E. Ruark
Cover designed by Sharon Wright

Printed in the United States of America

93 94 95 96 97 98 / DH / 10 9 8 7 6 5 4 3 2 1

CONTENTS

PREFACE TO THE SECOND EDITION

Eight years have passed since I first wrote this book, during which time I have conducted scores of divorce-recovery workshops and singles seminars in which I shared my ideas about friendship. It has been an enriching experience for me (and I hope, the participants), and has resulted in refinements that appear in this edition.

New to this edition is my chapter on singles' friendships. Over the years I have found that opposite-sex friendship is as fraught with difficulty for singles as it is for married people. Even same-sex relationships are problematic. Singles, nowadays, are developing new associations they call "family." These are intimates who are not biologically related to them. I have no objection to the development of emotional intimacies among singles. The problem I see for singles today is that they fail to see any difference between family and friends.

With family there is intimacy and a responsibility to carry the burden of intimacy—a responsibility to meet needs. The meeting of needs is an essential part of "family" life. But this is not true of friendship. Friends may meet one another's needs, but this is incidental to the friendship. Not so with intimacy and family. In fairness to singles, I must say that many times the biological family fails to meet needs. What then? Singles properly seek to have their needs met elsewhere. But in doing so it's important that they recognize that the relationships they establish in order to meet needs are more than friendships.

Another addition to this edition is my chapter called "The Friendship Test." It offers a simple and clear way to assess whether a relationship is friendship or whether it is something more.

My ideas about friendship are not original. I am indebted to C. S. Lewis's book *The Four Loves*. Lewis argues his case

7

for friendship as a philosopher. I argue his case as a professional counselor, offering guidance in developing friendships (particularly with the opposite sex) and pointing out the pitfalls.

Before we can answer the question, "Can men and women be just friends?" we need to determine what friendship is. Friendship in America has become something other than the noble virtue lauded by the ancients. It has become intimacy and is vested with a great deal of self-interest. Friends today look for love and affirmation. They are face-to-face occupied with each other and the emotional needs they expect to have met.

There is nothing wrong with love and affirmation, but this should not be confused with friendship. Given this new meaning of friendship, the potential trouble in opposite-sex relationships is evident. Whereas friendship was once incidental to the meeting of needs, today, friendship and need go together.

This book departs from most books on friendship by returning to the original meaning of friendship as conceived by the ancients and carried down through the history of Western man. Many books on friendship so-called tell us how to be more lovable and gain affirmation. But lovability and affirmation—"warm fuzzies," if you please—should not be confused with friendship. They have to do with psychological or emotional *need*. Friends are not *needed*, though life would be less enjoyable without them. They are *appreciated*, but not needed.

Intimacy and need-love are commitments belonging to family life—whether family of origin, a new family established by marriage, or a surrogate family established by singles based on mutual need. But intimacy and *need*-love always require commitment from others.

Before describing a relationship with someone of the opposite sex as being a "just friends" relationship, we do well to give friendship a second look. Is it really *friendship* we're talking about?

CHAPTER ONE
Just Friends

"Sure, you're *just* friends." Peggy's voice cut with sarcasm. Tim just sat there with a disgusted look on his face as if to say, "Here we go again."

Tim and Peggy had had a running battle over this issue for years—Tim's female friends. Tim, an aggressive tax attorney, was expanding his practice, but rather than take on a new attorney he had decided to promote his paralegal office manager, Rose, to legal assistant.

A very attractive, young, single woman, Rose had always been a source of uneasiness to Peggy. Whenever Peggy visited Tim's office, she just didn't like the way Rose looked at Tim as she talked to him. And Tim seemed embarrassed and flustered over Rose's obvious admiration in front of his wife.

What had brought Tim and Peggy to my office, according to Peggy, was that she had run out of patience. "Tim has been spending a lot of late nights at the office—alone with Rose. I haven't liked it, but I put up with it because Tim is building his practice and grooming Rose for her new position. But I have an uneasy feeling that a different kind of grooming is going on behind my back.

"I finally blew up when I found out late one night that Tim had taken Rose to a fancy restaurant for a candlelight dinner. But I had to drag it out of him. When he got home that night I asked him whether he had eaten supper. He said he had, but seemed uneasy about my question. So I asked where. He told me and acted even more uneasy. I kept prying and said, 'Pretty fancy, huh? What was the occasion?' He began to get defensive, and then I knew something was wrong. I said, 'Rose was with you, wasn't she?' He became angry, admitted she was, but said that he was not going to subject himself to a cross-examination by his wife when he was innocent of any wrong. 'Rose is just a valuable employee and friend,' he said, 'and that's that!'"

Both Tim and Peggy felt justified in taking the positions they had taken. Tim had no intention of getting a romance going with Rose. Only afterward did he realize that taking Rose to the fancy restaurant would raise questions in Peggy's mind.

Peggy thought Tim was being naïve. She felt that he didn't really understand women and that the "romantic setting" of the dinner might have encouraged what she perceived to be Rose's romantic interest in Tim.

What made the situation particularly alarming to Peggy—and made Tim look bad—was Tim's previous record with the opposite sex. Tim had a way of encouraging the attention of other women. It wasn't something that Peggy could put her finger on. It was more Tim's attitude. He seemed to give women the message: "Tell me I'm an attractive man." Whenever Peggy tried to talk to him about it, he would tell her she was silly and then refuse to discuss it further. Peggy was certain that Tim was encouraging Rose's attention.

NERVOUS HUSBANDS AND WIVES

Whether or not they should be, husbands and wives across the United States today are nervous about their spouses having opposite-sex friends. Practically every women's magazine has at some time run an article called "When Friends Become Lovers." A women's magazine ran an article that I'm sure agitated many women who find themselves in Peggy's circumstances. The article, entitled "A Matter of Convenience," said, "Professional women may have little time and energy for romance. Some find that a liaison with a married man leaves them free to climb the corporate ladder and satisfy their personal needs. . . ."[1]

The traditional homemaker like Peggy has always had these fears, justifiably. Female carnivores in the concrete jungle feel that married men are fair game.

But it's not only married men and single women who are changing sexual mores today. Married women are also. Over the past forty years, many married women have returned to the work force. In 1940, only 25.4 percent of the nation's women worked outside the home. Today 94.5 percent of men and 94.4 percent of women are employed![2]

This change in the social scene presents a problem that once was only the wife's concern. More and more, insecure husbands are wondering what their wives are doing at the office. They are beginning to feel and express the same doubt, suspicion, and distrust that wives traditionally have felt and expressed.

Fred, a pastor, is a case in point. His wife, Jill, works for their denominational publishing house.

"Something is wrong with my marriage, and I don't know what." Fred seemed confused and uneasy as he talked. "Jill has become very cold and distant, and when I ask her what's wrong she just says that she doesn't know. I've even wondered if another man is in the picture. On the one hand, I can't believe there is—Jill isn't the type to cheat. On the other hand, I wonder. Emotionally and sexually Jill wants nothing to do with me."

I asked Fred if he thought Jill would be willing to see me, and he thought she would. When I called her, she was quite willing to talk, and when we met she came right to the point.

"Fred can't understand why I want nothing to do with him, but I've told him again and again. He has no time for me. He is so wrapped up in his work that when he is at home he's physically and emotionally exhausted. I get from him what I've gotten my whole life—leftovers, crumbs.

"He doesn't need to worry that I'll divorce him. I'll just get on with my own life. I have a good job, and I have friends who care about me."

When Jill said "I have friends who care," she seemed uneasy about what she had said. It was hardly noticeable, and I would have dismissed it if she hadn't suddenly changed the subject and tried to dismiss the whole thing.

"I guess I'm just going through a low point in my life right now, and things will get better. We'll work things out." Her tone implied that she had said all she was going to say on the matter. It was the end of the conversation as far as she was concerned. So we sat in silence for a few minutes.

Finally I said, "Jill, a moment ago when you said that you have friends at work who care, you seemed uncomfortable about saying that."

Her eyes darted angrily. "You sound just like my supervisor. She told me the other day that she thought I spent too much time talking to Harry, one of my friends at work. The way she put it, you'd think that we were doing something immoral. I felt like Hester Prynne, complete with the big 'A' stitched in red."

We really got into it then. I suggested that if Harry were just a friend, she wouldn't be getting so defensive.

"I'll tell you why I'm defensive! All you religious goody-goodies are so hysterical about male-female relationships that you see evil in everything. I recall the Bible saying somewhere that only evil-minded people see evil in everything." She was steaming—and then she broke down in tears. I spent the rest of the session reestablishing rapport and helping her regain composure. She agreed to come back the following week and talk about it further.

True to her word, Jill returned. "I'm really confused." Her voice was flat, her face pale. "I haven't slept much this week. I keep going over and over in my mind, 'What's wrong with my friendship with Harry?' All we do is talk during break time and at lunch at the office. We have never gone out anywhere, even for lunch, or talked on the phone after hours. He has never touched me—not even to shake my hand.

"What's wrong with this friendship? Is it wrong for me to

feel that there is at least one person in life who understands me and cares? Is it wrong for a drowning person to grab hold of a life preserver and hang on for dear life? Yes, I know that's what I'm doing—I'm hanging on for dear life. If I hadn't had Harry's friendship, I think I'd have gone over the brink a long time ago. He's the only thing in life that makes it worth living."

The moment she said that, she again squirmed uneasily— the same kind of reaction I had seen a week earlier. She seemed to be saying, "I wish I hadn't said that." Then she said angrily, "Don't look at me like that! I've done nothing wrong!"

I said, "Don't lay it on me, Jill. You're condemning yourself. *I'm* not condemning you." Her tears came in torrents this time.

"It's wrong! I know it's wrong! I wish my husband could be more like Harry, and I'm angry at him because he's not. But I need Harry's friendship to survive! What can I do?"

Harry solved the problem for Jill. She decided to level with him about her feelings. She told him that he was the only bright spot in her life, that just talking to him lifted her spirits. She said she hoped that he was as fond of her as she was of him.

Fire blazed in Jill's eyes as she continued. "Do you know what he did? He acted as though he didn't know what I was talking about. He looked at me wide-eyed and innocent and said, 'I didn't know you felt that way!' That man was playing *games* with me. He was toying with my feelings! He knew full well how I felt and had led me to believe that he felt that way too. I had bared my soul to that man, and he acted as if there was nothing special about our relationship. Now I know what a woman must feel like after a one-night stand with a man who won't even talk with her the next day. I feel used!" Jill's infatuation had turned to fury.

FRIENDSHIP: A CONFUSING PHENOMENON

Jill is one of the reasons for this book's existence. There is much confusion over the subject of friendship, particularly opposite-sex friendship. Granted, most people feel that friendship is a wholesome and rewarding relationship between two people. However, when I ask the question, "Can men and women be just friends?" the reaction is varied.

Some respond, "Absolutely! It's only evil-minded people who raise their eyebrows at male-female friendships." When I suggest that opposite-sex friendships often turn out to be far more than that, the arguments are brushed aside. For some people, the rewards of a male-female friendship make it a risk worth taking.

Others respond, "Absolutely not!" Their sometimes unspoken thoughts are perhaps expressed by C. S. Lewis. Though he writes glowingly of the rewards of friendship, Lewis says that when two people of the opposite sex discover their friendship, it "will very easily pass—may pass in the first half-hour—into erotic love. Indeed, unless they are physically repulsive to each other or unless one or both already loves elsewhere, it is almost certain to do so sooner or later."[3]

Then there's a large group of confused, undecided people who simply don't know the answer to my question. A single mother told me, "I've given a great deal of thought to this question, and frankly, I'm confused. I do believe that male and female friends each offer a different perspective on things, just because they're male and female—like having male and female parents while growing up and learning about life. Their views complement one another.

"There are some things that I'd like to talk about with a male friend because I think the male point of view is valuable. For example, problems in raising my son. I'd love to have a male friend I could confide in and seek guidance from. But I'm reluctant to look for such a friend. I'd be mortified if a man thought that I might be trying to trap him into becoming a father to my son and a husband to me. So I do the next best thing: I go to a professional male therapist whose business it is to know such things and give me guidance. But I think it's a shame that men and women can't be just friends without feeling uncomfortable about it."

The majority of the people I talk to about opposite-sex friendships express the same kind of reservations this woman did. They simply cannot give unqualified approval to the idea. Others are confused, seeing both the rewards and the dangers. Still others are downright suspicious, believing that it's a risky business.

THE PROBLEM: A NEW KIND OF FRIENDSHIP

The problem couples face today with opposite-sex friendships can be understood only in light of the historical development of friendship. For most of the history of Western man, friendship was considered to be suitable for men only. But with the emancipation of women in the twentieth century, women were thought to be suitable candidates for friendships with men. Such a turn of events seems innocent enough and perhaps even healthy for the human race. But there's more to it.

IS IT REALLY FRIENDSHIP? At the time opposite-sex friendship became acceptable, the meaning of friendship began to change. Centuries ago the Greeks taught that there were three kinds of friendship, the highest being the selfless virtue of one person's acting with no other motive than the good of the other. There were two lesser friendships—the friendship of mutual advantage, in which friendship was pursued for mutual benefit; and the friendship of pleasure, in which the purpose was mutual enjoyment. Virtuous friendship was selfless. The other two types of friendship were vested with self-interest.

The Greeks, and most Western thinkers until the twentieth century, praised selfless friendship as being the only kind worthy of the word *friend*. But during this century the focus began to shift from selfless to self-interested friendship. A critical conjunction of events occurred. At the same time that opposite-sex friendship was gaining acceptance, friendship was also becoming narcissistic and self-seeking. It is easy to see the danger this posed—the pursuit of sexual gratification in the guise of friendship.

Though the danger was evident, modern man was in no mood to see it much less acknowledge it, and chose instead to ignore the danger and emphasize the positive features of opposite-sex friendship. Wasn't the emancipation of women a good thing? Wasn't friendship a good thing? What's wrong with putting these two good things together in opposite-sex friendship?

The argument for opposite-sex friendship is quite sound if friendship really is the virtuous, selfless ideal the Greeks and great Western thinkers had in mind. But it is not. It is vested with self-interest.

PLATO IS ALIVE AND WELL. While these changes were taking place earlier in this century, another force was at work, complicating things even further. This force is grounded in an interesting Greek philosophy of male-female relations that modern man has adopted. It is known historically as Neoplatonism.

Greek men who wished to be virtuous faced the problem of how they could retain their virtue and also cope with their sexual attraction for women. They came up with a clever solution: Separate the mind (ideas) from the body (passion). That is, if a man has sexual relations with a woman but dismisses it as merely a passionate act—meaningless as far as the mind is concerned—he will retain his virtue. As a result, the Greek male spoke in terms of possessing a woman while not being possessed by her.

That is what modern men and women usually do when their friendships get sexual. They simply dismiss sex as being meaningless, an expression of passion that has no implication beyond mere recreation.

This attitude was forcefully illustrated in a 1971 Dustin Hoffman movie called, *Who Is Harry Kellerman and Why Is He Saying All Those Terrible Things About Me?* Hoffman played Georgie, a discontented folk-rock composer trying to come to terms with himself.

In one scene, Georgie holds an audition for singers, and one of them is a thirty-four-year-old woman who is as lost as he is. In fact, she's an emotional wreck. She doesn't even make it through the audition. Feeling a kindred spirit of lostness, Georgie takes her home with him. After a few glasses of wine, the woman tells Georgie that she appreciates his attention. Only that morning she had considered taking her life. But now things look a lot better—at least momentarily. She is grateful for Georgie's kindness. He is a "true friend."

Both talk about the frustrations and heartaches of the past. They agree that the wine and the company they are sharing seem nice by contrast.

Eventually the question is raised, Will they go to bed together? Yes, Georgie's friend says she'd like that. But she assures him that she won't tell him she loves him. She has found that the moment she talks about love with men, they can't get away from her fast enough. So, yes, they'll have sex. But, no, he doesn't need to worry about words of love. A one-night stand—that's all it will be.

Modern man treats sexual relations outside of marriage exactly as the Greeks did. He is able to get on with his life, totally indifferent to sexual relations, because sex means nothing.

Friendship as practiced today is seldom like the virtuous friendships of the past. On the surface this may appear to be an important advance in male-female relations. Women have been emancipated. Opposite-sex friendship is declared possible. But a little probing beneath the surface reveals that we're not talking about the virtue the Greeks and Western civilization once knew, but rather a relationship heavy with self-interest. What is more, modern man's view of his sexuality is flawed. We tend to think of sexuality in terms of what we *do* rather than what we *are*—male and female, with all the richness that difference offers. By reverting to Neoplatonism and reducing sex to a meaningless act, we have lost a great deal of what God has given us as creatures created male and female.

These are the issues behind the troubled condition of opposite-sex friendships today. Given this state of affairs, couples are asking the question: Is an opposite-sex friendship outside of marriage possible?

Single people are asking about opposite-sex friendship too. Whether they are electing to remain single or are open to marriage, they find that opposite-sex friendships so-called are a mine field—as the 1990 film *When Harry Met Sally* attests. Harry's observation that sex tends to get in the way of friendship between men and women strikes a realistic note for many singles.

Can men and women be just friends? In order to answer this we must consider what true friendship really is.

CHAPTER TWO
What Is Friendship?

Americans want friends. The book *How To Win Friends and Influence People*, with sales in the millions, is testimony to that fact. Another book, *The Friendship Factor* by Alan L. McGinniss, has sold over a half-million copies.

These books touch Americans where they hurt—in interpersonal relationships—but they are not books about friendship. They teach us how to get close to the people we love and how to give and get affirmation. They offer legitimate techniques that can make us more lovable. However, these books do us a disservice by making us think we are experiencing friendship when we are actually experiencing affection, affirmation, or intimacy. None of these is friendship.

FRIENDS ARE DISCOVERED, NOT MADE

Historically people's goals have not been to make friends. Friendship has been secondary, growing out of discovery—the discovery of kindred spirits who see things alike.

THE LOVE OF TWO GREAT WARRIORS. The Old Testament story of David and Jonathan is one example of discovery friendship. Like many others through the ages, David and Jonathan discovered each other during a time of war. Israel was fighting the Philistines, and Jonathan, King Saul's son, was a courageous warrior. He and his armor bearer had fought twenty Philistines and had killed them all (1 Sam. 14:14).

David became famous by killing the Philistine giant Goliath (1 Sam. 17). The two warriors met as David triumphantly returned to Jerusalem carrying Goliath's head. When Jonathan saw David, his fighting instincts were awakened. He must have said to himself, "There is a man who knows what this war is all about!"

Jonathan discovered in David another warrior as fearless and as dedicated to the cause of Israel as was he. In the midst of the horror of war Jonathan was suddenly drawn to David. The historian says, "the soul of Jonathan was knit to the soul of David, and Jonathan loved him as himself" (1 Sam. 18:1).

Those who have been through war and other tragedies that try men's souls have experienced this affinity. It's as though they discover another self—another person who champions the same cause and fights for it with equal vigor and skill.

FRIENDSHIP MUST BE ABOUT SOMETHING. What made the friendship between these two warriors true and binding is that it was *about* something. David and Jonathan had some things in common—a hatred for the Philistines and a war to win. And each admired the other's ability as a warrior.

People who want friends seldom find them because the very condition of having friends is that we should want something else.[1] Friendship involves two or more people who suddenly discover that they see things the same way. They share the same view of things. Unless friendship's about something, there is no friendship. The words of C. S. Lewis affirm this.

> *[If] the truthful answer to the question* Do you see the same truth? *would be "I see nothing, and I don't care about the truth; I only want a Friend," no Friendship can arise—though affection of course may. There would be nothing for the Friendship to be about;*

and Friendship must be about something even if it were only an enthusiasm for dominoes or white mice. Those who have nothing can share nothing; those who are going nowhere can have no fellow-travelers.[2]

When two people find out that they see things in the same way, they have *discovered* a friend.

Lewis' distinction between friendship and affection is important. These are different kinds of love, and we must not confuse one experience for another. We sometimes claim that we're talking about friendship when we're really talking about something else, such as affection.

Affection involves "need-love," both the need to give and the need to receive. The needs may be emotional or physical. They may be the need to give and get words of affirmation or to give and get physical affection. But in either case, the giving and getting—the need-love—is the paramount thing.

In recent years this phenomenon in its neurotic form has been called "co-dependency." Two people can be locked together in a need to give and get, which eventually destroys the relationship and warps them as individuals. They never become peers or equals (which is found in friendship) because the giver must (for a continual sense of security and worth) forever give and require nothing from the significant other. The significant other must (for continuing security and worth) maintain a posture of helplessness, able to do little or nothing for self and needing virtually everything from the giver. The co-dependent relationship remains like that of parent to a child. The child never grows up, nor can he or she afford to because then the mutuality of need would be broken.

In its healthy form, need-love is beautiful and part of the human experience that binds people together. But it is not to be confused with friendship.

MARTI WANTS FRIENDS. Marti, a college junior, was depressed. She had just been through a painful love affair and felt caught between a need to lick her wounds and a need for people. She was surrounded by people all day at school, but she still felt lonely. How was she to find friends?

Let's pretend that she's in class one day, and Professor Whatnabble—who frequently assigns stupid, meaningless work to the class—hands out another dumb assignment. Her stomach goes into a knot. She wants to say something, but everyone else in the room remains silent—except for a male student across the room. When he hears the assignment, he tilts back in his chair, throws back his head, rolls his eyes, and breaks his pencil in half. The professor looks disgustedly at the nonconformist and returns to the business at hand. But Marti has discovered a friend.

If she finds the courage, she'll go to the student after class and say, "I'm glad to know I'm not the only one who feels Professor Whatnabble hands out dumb assignments. I appreciate your bravery in expressing your feelings. I wish we could do something about the problem."

If this were a storybook, a friendship would start, and the two of them would take on Professor Whatnabble, perhaps the academic dean, and maybe the entire administration. Whether or not that happens, the seeds of friendship have been sown. Marti had made a *discovery*. There was someone who saw things the way she did. Her loneliness was dispelled by a feeling of affinity with this person. She appreciated his willingness to communicate what she felt needed to be expressed.

Lewis speaks to this point.

> The typical expression of opening Friendship would be something like, "What? You too? I thought I was the only one." We can imagine that among those early hunters and warriors single individuals—one in a century? one in a thousand years?—saw what others did not; saw that the deer was beautiful as well as edible, that hunting was fun as well as necessary, dreamed that his gods might be not only powerful but holy. But as long as each of these percipient persons dies without finding a kindred soul, nothing

(I suspect) will come of it; art of sport or spiritual religion will not be born. It is when two such persons discover one another, when, whether with immense difficulties and semi-articulate fumbling or with what would seem to us amazing elliptical speed, they share their vision—it is then that Friendship is born. And instantly they stand together in an immense solitude.[3]

Americans have trouble with opposite-sex friendships because often these relationships are not friendships at all. A man and a woman may have some common interests, but that's not what draws them together. They are drawn together by their interest in *each other* and the affirmation they give each other.

Affirmation is fine. But let's call it that. When one spouse is concerned about what's going on in certain relationships, the other ought to be honest and not reply defensively, "We're just friends." If that defense is offered, spouses should ask, "Well then, what is the friendship *about?*" If it's friendship, it must be about something besides each other. Friends are side by side looking ahead at their common interest. Lovers are face-to-face looking at each other and occupied with their feelings for each other. Again, Lewis says:

> though we can have erotic love and friendship for the same person yet in some ways nothing is less like Friendship than a love-affair. Lovers are always talking to one another about their love; Friends hardly ever about their Friendship. Lovers are normally face-to-face, absorbed in each other; Friends are side by side absorbed in some common interest.[4]

I don't mean to imply (nor does Lewis) that there is no bond between friends. The bond that is between lovers is of a different character than is the bond between friends.

The bond between friends, which rises out of a common vision, is tested with each step they take together. And as each person rises to the occasion, reliance, respect, and admiration for one another blossom into appreciative-love.

Without the vision and the struggle to realize it there would be no knowledge of the friend. It is in struggling together that we come to know the friend as he could not otherwise be known. Lewis says:

> *You will not find the warrior, the poet, the philosopher or the Christian by staring in his eyes as if he were your mistress: better fight beside him, read with him, argue with him, pray with him.*[5]

We know this intuitively. The worried husband whose wife has a "friendship" with a male co-worker at the office knows the difference between a bond that comes from working together and the bond that comes from looking into each other's eyes.

The single young woman who wants to remain single (or at least is very choosy about candidates for marriage) knows the difference between the bond that comes from enjoying common interests with a man and the bond that comes from looking into each other's eyes.

TWO IS NOT THE NECESSARY NUMBER

Marti's discovery of friends might be just beginning. For two, far from being the necessary number for friendship, isn't even the best. The two would be happily joined by a third or a fourth. I can imagine Marti and her friend outside the classroom discussing their new discovery—their mutual feelings about Professor Whatnabble. As they talk, another student from the class walks by and overhears them. He stops to listen and discovers quite by accident that these people feel as he does! The two are joined by a third student and perhaps later a fourth. As they talk, their feelings of isolation begin to fade. At one time each of these students felt alone. Now they are uniting and establishing a mutual identity.

Friendship so-called—particularly opposite-sex friendship—is often exclusive: just two. We can easily find out if a relationship is friendship or something more intimate by suggesting that the twosome make it a threesome. Lovers want privacy. Friends, drawn together by their common interest, would gladly reduce that solitude. They welcome others of like mind; there is strength in numbers. As the number of friends increases, they find an increase in pleasure. Eros has no such interest. We willingly share our friends, but not our lovers. C. S. Lewis says:

> If, of three friends (A, B, and C) A should die, then B loses not only A but "A's part in C," while C loses not only A but "A's part in B." In each of my friends there is something that only some other friend can fully bring out. By myself I am not large enough to call the whole man into activity; I want other lights than my own to show all his facets. Now that Charles is dead, I shall never again see Ronald's reaction to a specifically Caroline joke. Far from having more of Ronald, having him "to myself" now that Charles is away, I have less of Ronald. Hence true Friendship is the least jealous of loves. Two friends delight to be joined by a third, and three by a fourth, if only the newcomer is qualified to become a real friend.[6]

There is, however, a sense in which friends enjoy solitude, but it is not the same solitude enjoyed by those who share the need-love of affection. The solitude of friends is "we" against "them." The we may be two, but the two are always willing to admit others and strengthen their faction against them.

On the other hand, those who have a need-love for each other are reluctant to admit others into the relationship. Someone else may interfere with the giving and getting of need.

I see no evil in a need-love relationship being unwilling to jeopardize itself by admitting others to it. But when we are clear about the nature of the relationship and maintain necessary distinctions (and boundaries), we run much less risk of being hurt or of hurting others through misunderstandings. We will not make the mistake of calling a need-love relationship a friendship.

Friends certainly will meet one another's needs as they arise, particularly in times of sickness and death. But as C. S. Lewis says:

> *Such good offices are not the stuff of Friendship. The occasions for them are almost interruptions. They are in one way relevant to it, in another not. Relevant, because you would be a false friend if you would not do them when the need arose; irrelevant, because the role of benefactor always remains accidental, even a little alien, to that of Friend. It is almost embarrassing. For Friendship is utterly free from Affection's need to be needed.*[7]

COMPANIONSHIP IS NOT THE SAME AS FRIENDSHIP

While we may have some friends who are closer to us than other friends (often referred to by the words *friends* and *best friends*) we should not make the mistake of calling someone a friend who really is a companion. We must distinguish friendship not only from affection and eros, but also from companionship. Companionship is found among people who do things together for enjoyment or survival. Friendship involves admiration over the *way* they do things together.

For example, hunters or warriors find in their cooperative effort enjoyment and survival. "Talking shop" is an enjoyable pastime. The hunter recreates the scene and recounts how he flushed his quarry and went for the kill. The other hunters relive the excitement, speculating on how it might have been done more efficiently if the terrain had been used differently or a lighter spear had been chosen. These people are companions and their connection should not be confused with friendship.

Lewis says, "Palaeolithic man may not have had a club on his shoulder, but he certainly had a club of the other sort."[8]

This "clubbableness," as Lewis calls it, is companionship. There is enjoyment in it as well as survival value.

Companions can become friends. We can see this happen between foxhole buddies. Their survival depends on an effective, cooperative effort. They may sit around the mess tent with their other buddies after it's all over and relive the fight. But friends will be expressing a certain admiration or appreciation for the *way* the battle was fought. The battle was only the matrix in which the unique qualities of a person were revealed. *Friendship is the appreciation of these qualities.* This is what happened between Jonathan and David.

Of course, friends will be allies, but not because they are friends. Being allies has more to do with the survival of comrades in the same conflict. When one saves the other's life, the attitude of an ally is, "Don't mention it." Survival has nothing to do with friendship. If they weren't friends, they would still protect each other in the interest of survival. The message is, "I don't need *you* to survive. I need somebody to fight the enemy with me, but not necessarily *you*. But, having fought the enemy with you, having stood shoulder to shoulder with you, I have come to *appreciate* your style as a warrior."

Friendship has nothing to do with *need* or being *needed*. Beware of people who talk about "needing" friends. They probably need something else. Companionship has to do with wanting *someone* for survival or *someone* with whom to pass the time, though not necessarily *you*. For survival or a pleasant pastime, a companion will find someone else if you're not available.

When two companions discover a kindred spirit and develop an appreciation for each other—a friendship—they will cultivate each other. They may lunch together or enjoy a social occasion together. But the basis of their attraction is not mutual *need*. The attraction is their common interest, which becomes the matrix for friendship.

Not all companionship or even friendship is benign, however, even with the same sex. Consider the gang in

Proverbs who say, "Come along with us; . . . let's waylay some harmless soul" (Prov. 1:11 NIV). We are concerned when a child or spouse socializes with people who are bad influences. We don't object so much to their having companions, having fun, or even discovering friends. The problem lies in the type of people or the activities involved. Married couples often disagree over activities or friendships because the type of activity or the people involved may simply be unwholesome.

We must willingly respect that need for security and choose companions and activities accordingly. A need for unwholesome people and activities is a legitimate cause of concern for our spouses.

COMPANIONS, FRIENDS, AND LOVERS

The difference between companions, friends, and lovers may be illustrated by diagrams.

COMPANIONS.

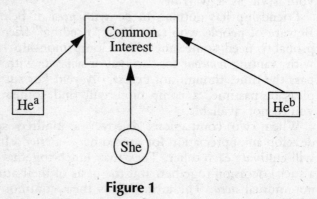

Figure 1

In Figure 1, three people are drawn together by a common interest. They engage in some cooperative effort and have limited social contact. They may even be sociable with each other, but that's the extent of it.

FRIENDS.

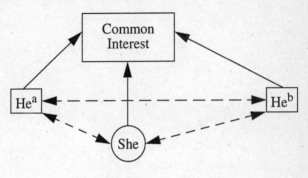

Figure 2

One day, in the context of their common interest (the solid lines, Figure 2), the companions discover that they look at it (common interest) as no one else does. There is a "What? You too?" sensation. In my imaginary story this is what started with Marti in the classroom and continued in the hall. A discovery was made. Two people saw the same truth. As they watched each other in the context of their common interest (or truth) they appreciated each other more and more. The unique way another person talks and acts results in appreciation.

Let's suppose that He^a is an abrasive person who handles Professor Whatnabble in a very direct, discourteous manner. But He^b is very gentle and courteous and seems to get a lot further with the professor. He^a appreciates He^b for the contribution made to his understanding of how to handle people. He^b, who tends to be timid, may appreciate He^a for his ability to stand up for himself. He^b draws a lot of courage from He^a. The same kind of exchange goes on between He^a and He^b and She. This appreciation is represented by the dashes in Figure 2.

In time He[b] notices that the friendship of the three is beginning to change.

LOVERS. The character of the friendship begins to look like figure 3.

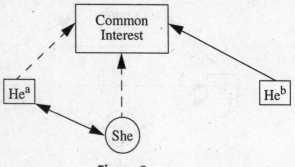

Figure 3

He[a] and She are no longer shoulder to shoulder facing a common interest with He[b]. That has become secondary (dashes, Figure 3). He[a] and She are now face-to-face, occupied with *each other* (solid line). He[b] is still focused on the common interest (solid line), but feels cut off from He[a] and She because they are no longer occupied with the same interest. He[b] is still doing battle with Professor Whatnabble, but He[a] and She are now occupied with each other. What has happened? *Three friends have become two lovers.*

This kind of change was affecting Tim and Peggy and Fred and Jill in chapter 1. It made them wonder, "Is this other person just a friend?" Several questions can be asked to test the friendship.

First, are all the parties who are involved occupied with a mutual interest? Is this interest their primary concern? Is their appreciation for each other an outgrowth of this interest and sustained by it? Or, do any of them pair off and show by their behavior that they are more interested in each other than in their common interest?

Second, is the pairing off designed to make the relationship exclusive? Have they narrowed the friendship down to include just the two of them, or is a third party welcomed? Satisfactory answers to these questions will give rest to the minds of worried husbands and wives.

APPRECIATIVE-LOVE VS. NEED-LOVE

True friendship is appreciative-love. It is appreciation for the other person in the context of a legitimate interest. A true friend is not needed as a source of emotional fulfillment. The person may be a source of appreciation, but that person isn't *needed*. When emotional *need* is revealed, alarm bells go off. Consider the following illustration:

A wine connoisseur has a particular liking for good claret. He is a man whose palate knows a good claret when he tastes it. His sense of beauty demands that he use a fine crystal decanter and goblet whenever he drinks. He pours the claret, smells it, and looks admiringly at its color. He is in no hurry to consume it. He savors each sip.

One day his wife notices a change in his behavior. When he goes for the claret he doesn't use his crystal goblet, but pours a large draft into a plain drinking glass instead. He seems to care little about the claret's bouquet or color; he gulps it down instead of sipping it.

His wife says nothing, but during the following days and weeks she notices that this behavior continues and that he returns to the decanter for refills. Then one day she discovers that he has been sneaking drinks from a secretly stashed bottle. Her husband has been transformed from an *appreciative connoisseur* to a man who *needs a drink.*

APPRECIATIVE-LOVE. Appreciation is no problem. But when appreciation turns to need, it is often cause for alarm. When a person has a need for someone outside of marriage, it raises an important question for the spouse: "What's missing in the marriage that prompts such a need?"

Friendship as appreciative-love is quite properly pursued

outside of marriage. It is a human experience which, though not necessary, makes our lives richer. As I think back on same- and opposite-sex friendships I have had, I'm aware that I didn't *need* them. But my life would be poorer without them.

NEED-LOVE. Need-love views the loved one differently. The needed person is seen in relation to us just as the claret is seen by the alcoholic. The sad thing about need-love is that it lasts only as long as there is a need. This is why Aristotle called such friendships "incidental": they are easily dissolved if the other party is no longer pleasant or useful.

This doesn't mean that all affections that begin as need-love are transitory. The need may be permanent or recurrent and therefore guarantee the perpetuation of need-love. It may even be sealed by the commitment of marriage and fidelity. But it is easily dissolved. C. S. Lewis says:

> Where need-love is left unaided we can hardly expect it not to "die on us" once the need is no more. That is why the world rings with the complaints of mothers whose grown-up children neglect them and of forsaken mistresses whose lovers' love was pure need—which they have satisfied.[9]

TERRY'S HEARTBREAK. Terry offers a good example of need-love that died. Terry was a woman in her early thirties, married for ten years, who had no feelings left for her husband. It didn't surprise me when she said she had been sexually involved with a "friend" at the office.

She had become pregnant without her husband's knowledge. When she had found out about the pregnancy she had gone out and had an abortion and kept the truth from her husband. But that wasn't her problem either.

The real problem was with her friend, the father of the child. When he had heard that she was pregnant, he no longer wanted anything to do with her. He had no interest or concern over the abortion and became very cool toward her. What made matters worse was that he was beginning to date her girlfriend, who worked in the same office. Terry was crushed.

Need-love, left unaided, was all over when Terry's male friend decided that she had outlived her usefulness. Appreciative-love, by contrast, is the virtuous friendship Aristotle wrote about. It is a disinterested or unselfish love. It is a value placed on the loved person. The person is admired but not used. Lewis says:

> It is the feeling which would make a man unwilling to deface a great picture even if he were the last man left alive and himself about to die; which makes us glad of unspoiled forests that we shall never see; which makes us anxious that the garden or bean-field should continue to exist. We do not merely like the things; we pronounce them, in a momentary God-like sense, "very good."[10]

Do we draw the conclusion that a man should be able to have an appreciative-love for a beautiful woman as a thing of beauty? Perhaps, if it's at a beauty pageant. But if he claims her as a friend, he had better have a more substantial interest than her beauty—which takes us back to friendship being *about* something other than the persons involved.

It is possible for a married man to have a beautiful woman (other than his wife) as a friend, if the friendship is about something besides her beauty. Though her beauty cannot be ignored, it might be appreciated as something quite disconnected from any personal interest. She would be beautiful whether or not he said so. But her beauty is not seen in connection with his own interest.

When I was a pastor I had two beautiful, well-groomed women working for me in the office. I appreciated the fact that we had such a "good face" to present to the public. I appreciated the fact that being a Christian needn't make one look ugly or dowdy. But their beauty had nothing to do with my own personal interest.

There are two issues, then: First, is the friendship *about* something? Second, does the husband show a disinterested love—that is, pure appreciation? Given that assurance, his wife will most likely rest easy. No doubt the wife will keep an eye on the woman to make sure *she* returns no more than disinterested love.

This was Peggy's problem in chapter 1. When she watched Rose, she didn't see a disinterested love—mere appreciation for Tim. She saw Rose light up with an inner glow that suggested much more. She knew Tim was getting the message, because he acted so ill at ease.

When a man and woman do not behave as thirsty people driven to each other by some unspoken need, they probably won't provoke questions about their relationship. They behave more like the connoisseur enjoying his claret, quite willing to put it aside if it appears that appreciation is turning to need.

IS FRIENDSHIP EVER PURE? Defining friendship as appreciative-love and contrasting it with need-love is important to my analysis of the subject. When we analyze something we say "it is this," and "it is not that."

We should not conclude, however, that friendship given with pure intent may not later have some impure elements of self-interest mixed in. There are those who seriously doubt that friendship as I describe it is possible at all.

Samuel Johnson is one such skeptic. In his *Life of Johnson,* Boswell tells Johnson of a wealthy lady who did good for many people, but he left her motive open to question. She was in no way secretive about her benevolence and seemed quite self-satisfied when her good deeds were made known.

To this, Johnson replies that he has never seen anyone act from pure benevolence, whether in heaven or earth. "No, Sir; to act from pure benevolence is not possible for finite beings. Human benevolence is mingled with vanity, interest, or some other motive."[11]

Perhaps Johnson is right. Even those of us who believe our motive is pure benevolence often discover later that it was contaminated with self-interest. We have an incredible ability to deceive ourselves and others even in doing good. It may be helpful, therefore, to see friendship on a continuum from pure appreciative-love (if it exists in pure form) to pure need-love (Figure 4).

Appreciative-
love

Need-
love

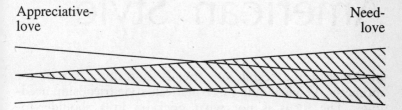

Figure 4

Such a view of friendship may, in the long run, have a wholesome effect on both the friend and the befriended. It may keep us from thinking more highly of ourselves than we ought to think and guard us from spiritual pride that says, "I thank thee, God, that I am not as other men."

CHAPTER THREE
Friendship American Style

In America the search for friends is really a search for intimates. Lewis would call American-style friendship need-love. The focus is not what goes on in a shoulder-to-shoulder relationship. The focus is on each other in a face-to-face relationship. Having an intimate talk and sharing intimate aspects of their personal lives is what people want to do today when they are with friends.

To the contemporary American, intimacy is not necessarily sexual, though it may become that. Some intimacy is purely emotional. But no matter how it is cast, whether sexual or emotional or both, the overwhelming theme of friendship among Americans is intimacy.

FRIENDSHIP AS INTIMACY

Intimacy has been defined as "close personal interaction that is marked by mutuality, emotional accessibility, endurance in time and the possibility of being known multidimensionally."[1] The quest for intimacy in America is largely because of the loss of intimacy, which was once gained through marriage and family.[2] In the feudal era, family life and loyalty governed the social, political, and economic life of the individual. It provided him with escape from loneliness and isolation. It offered an opportunity for self-expression and social support. It relieved him of always having to wear an acceptable public image. He could be himself with his family, with all his physical, psychological, and social liabilities—within limits. His family accepted and loved him, though others might not.[3]

During the Renaissance and the Reformation, the individuality of humanity blossomed. The creative artist and the merchant-trader, able to function socially, politically, and economically apart from the family came into being. But the individual paid a price for his individuality. He gave up his support system, the family, unless he chose to marry and establish a new support system—a family of his own.

The individual thus faced a dilemma—his desire for the intimacy of family life, and the price he had to pay for it. The price was a certain *burden* of intimacy. In exchange for family support, the family demanded commitment and a certain suspension of self-centeredness for the sake of others in the family.[4]

INTIMACY WITHOUT THE BURDEN OF INTIMACY. Over the years the desire for both autonomy and a support group kept the individual in tension. He continually invented social institutions, both formal and informal, designed to maximize emotional support and minimize the loss of autonomy. These institutions have taken the form of fraternal organizations, country and social clubs, singles bars, condominiums, street gangs, bohemian neighborhoods, and the cliques and peer groups that are formed in large corporations. The communal movement of the sixties with its open and group marriages is the result of this attempt to have intimacy without also having the burden of intimacy.[5] In short, autonomous man wants it both ways. He wants his freedom, but he wants the intimacy offered by social involvement with others.

Friendship as intimacy is a modern social form attempting to do just this. It seeks shelter from the expectations of the public and freedom to express one's self in an accepting environment. It also looks for social support, tolerance, trust, affection, and love. But it goes further. It seeks intimacy without accepting the *burden* of intimacy that is to be found in family life.

Although Americans talk about commitment, intimate relationships (I won't call them friendships) rarely survive when the two people are no longer useful to each other. True commitment acts with no reward in mind. It is the stuff that holds families together—parents and children, husbands and wives. It is a loyalty that we owe the family. It's the nature of the bond.

If you crowd someone in an intimate relationship, which you call friendship, that relationship will not last. This is why friendship (so-called) in America today is so troubled. *It is intimacy without the burden of intimacy.*

This is the kind of friendship Aristotle called "incidental." It is not true friendship. He was right when he said that such friendships are easily dissolved, because if one party ceases to be pleasant or useful, the other ceases to love.

It seems odd that this should be called intimacy at all. If intimacy means "close personal interaction marked by mutuality, emotional accessibility, endurance in time and the possibility of being known multidimensionally," it is hard to think of friendship as an opportunity to enjoy intimacy without being burdened by its responsibility either in the commitment of marriage or in commitment to a surrogate family through formal or informal adoption.

Friendship American style is psychological *coitus interruptus* (contraception by withdrawal). This illustration is used not to titillate, but to draw an analogy.

Two people are becoming emotionally involved. They are experiencing a great number of intimate feelings. They are not married and do not intend to be. Nor do they want to take on "the burden of intimacy" that family life imposes. Therefore, they have no alternative other than to break off the relationship. There is no future in a relationship that does not accept the burden of intimacy. People think that they can have psychological intercourse without accepting the burden of it. But even psychological intercourse cannot be fully satisfied without the commitment that goes with it.

This is why many so-called friendships end when one friend begins to have expectations of the other. The emotional or perhaps physical intimacy of the friendship means that there is some kind of commitment. But commitment connotes burden, and the modern American accepts no burden with intimacy.

The unfettered nature of friendship is explicit in the very etymology of the word *friend*. The Germanic and Celtic roots of the words *friend* and *free* are the same. The friend was distinguished from the slave, who was not free. The slave acted solely out of obligation. The free man acted out of no obligation and was, therefore, called by the Old English word *fréon*—a friend.[6]

There is reciprocity in friendship. But true friendship does not involve reciprocal *intimacy*. The line is drawn at intimacy. Any attempt to carry friendship into intimacy is properly refused by a friend. A true friend cares enough about the other friend not to offer the opportunity for intimacy.

This is why male-female relationships among unmarried youth traditionally were watched closely. A number of social safeguards kept youth from getting involved intimately. When a young man showed interest in a young woman, she was to bring him home to meet her parents. Father would ask the question, "Young man, just what are your intentions toward my daughter?" If he wanted to date her, then approved or chaperoned activities were arranged to monitor the progress of the relationship. If they were "serious" about each other and were considering marriage, an engagement was announced and a protocol went along with that. When they were certain of marriage, they were married, and the barriers to intimacy were removed.

Why all these barriers? Historically we believed that intimacy without commitment was not only morally wrong, but destructive to the individual and to society. The lack of restraint during the past forty years has proven our earlier beliefs to be correct.

Friendship American style looks for emotional and often physical intimacy without the burden of an enduring commitment. We wrongly suppose that we can go just so far and then stop. But this is to seek the impossible. Intimacy, both emotional and sexual, is of a nature that we *should* go all the way. Because of this, the burdens of intimacy are unavoidable. This is why historically we insisted on chaperons, engagement, and the commitment of marriage when two people wanted intimacy.

Parents need to supervise the opposite-sex relations of their teenage children. The wise parent isn't drawn in with "Don't you trust me?" The proper parental response is "Trust has nothing to do with it. In fact, I would expect you to do what comes naturally. I hope that I have raised you to be a red-blooded heterosexual who has strong desires for emotional and sexual intimacy with the opposite sex. It's because I believe you are a red-blooded heterosexual that I *expect* your emotional and sexual instincts to be excited. Because of those expectations, I don't want to see you get caught in a compromising situation where you will have an opportunity to do what comes naturally."

Parental concerns are not limited to sexual involvement. Teenagers can become so *emotionally* involved with the opposite sex that their emotional and psychological growth is stunted. I have seen young men so tied down by girlfriends that they give up their male friendships and activities. But they are not psychologically or socially ready to make such commitments. They need the freedom to become fully developed, independent adults before they choose to give up independence for the commitments intimacy requires.

Americans are alarmed over an environment damaged by chemicals and nuclear waste. Yet hundreds of thousands of people are being damaged by a social disease that is actually encouraged: intimacy without the burden of total commitment.

Friendship American style is unrealistic. Indeed, it's insane. Two people who begin to rely on each other for their intimacy needs are setting the stage for heartbreak if they do not have adequate rules to guard their physical and emotional welfare.

This caused Terry's heartbreak. Her male friend was willing to be intimate with her until confronted with an illegitimate pregnancy. He wanted nothing to do with that burden of intimacy.

It was this false intimacy that psychoanalyst Erik Erickson had in mind when he said:

> Some people today may fool themselves in their so-called recreational sexuality and actually feel quite isolated because they lack mutuality—real intimacy. In extreme cases, you could have a highly active sex life and yet feel a terrible sense of isolation because you're never there as a person; you're never perceiving your partner as a person. Real intimacy includes the capacity to commit yourself to relationships that may demand sacrifice and compromise.[7]

THE MODERN NEOPLATONIST. Intimacy without the burden of intimacy is an idea that the ancient Greek Neoplatonists would heartily endorse. They would say, "Now you have it. You can go as far as you want with intimacy, as long as you remain a free, autonomous individual."

Modern man does not have the same religious motive the Greeks had—to remain virtuous, while at the same time satisfying the desires for emotional and sexual intimacy. But he is following Greek tradition by attempting to be autonomous while enjoying all the benefits of relations with other people. *Possess the woman; but don't be possessed by her!*

Friendship American style has managed to preserve the worst of Greek tradition. It has preserved the Neoplatonic

autonomous man and the least valuable forms of friendship—friendships of interest and pleasure.

THE FAILURE OF OPEN MARRIAGE. A prime example of
intimacy without the burden of intimacy was America's
experiment with "open marriage." In 1972 Nena and
George O'Neill's book *Open Marriage* was hailed as an
alternative to the oppressive roles and rules of traditional
marriage. In the book, couples were told that they were free
to exercise their wills separately, which could include having
social, intellectual, and sexual activity outside the marriage.
In short, intimacy without the burden of intimacy.

By 1978 there was ample evidence that the experiment had
failed. Nena O'Neill reported that among the 250 open-
marriage couples she had studied, those relationships that
ended within two years tended to be ones that included some
planned extramarital sex.[8]

Sexual infidelity is not the only problem. Opposite-sex
intimacy without sexual activity is also a source of trouble
for married couples. Many married people feel that sharing
an emotional and intellectual bond with someone else is
really a deeper intimacy than sex. Marriage counselors Leota
and Robert Tucker put it this way:

> *People in love just don't want to share their mates; they are
> threatened by cross-sex intimacy even where there is no explicit
> sexual contact. They want their committed relationship to be
> special; when that special link is threatened, they become jealous.
> Intimate cross-sex friendships involve that close, private familiarity
> and warmth that is the core of the committed relationship.*[9]

Emotional and intellectual intimacy with a third party erodes
the security a person seeks in marriage. Married couples
share a special intimacy, which they trust will be exclusive.

One of the things that made Peggy furious about Tim's
friendship with Rose was that Rose seemed to know so
much about their private lives. Rose knew how Peggy felt
about her mother-in-law and even the fact that Peggy wore

socks to bed to keep her feet warm! Peggy wanted to know *what else* Tim had told Rose about their private lives!

Some would argue that Peggy is guilty of ridiculous, old-fashioned jealousy that interferes with personal freedom and growth. But jealousy should not be dismissed so quickly. I deal with this in chapter 9. This much should be said here: Jealousy is not an unwholesome emotion. It is a proper response to a threatened love relationship. Jealousy indicates that a value is placed on that relationship. A lack of jealousy may indicate a weak love bond.

God repeatedly spoke through the Old Testament prophets of his jealousy over Israel. He was jealous for his chosen people who had turned their backs on him (Zech. 1:14; 8:2).

The Tuckers say:

> *A cross-sex third party, whether lover or friend, is a potential threat to confidentiality and exclusivity. The excluded partner may believe (rightly or wrongly) that confidentiality is being violated by the cross-sex friendship. The resulting distrust, and the sense that privacy is being invaded, can make the one left out fear being replaced. If the other partner continues the cross-sex friendship it's likely to become clandestine. Then a separate set of intimacies and understandings could arise. This parallel relationship may compete with the primary relationship, leading to considerable stress and conflict. Besides increasing tension and conflict in the committed relationship, cross-sex friendships may also provide an option that reduces one partner's motivation to struggle with normal relationship problems. This weakens the committed relationship and creates the possibility that the cross-sex relationship may supplant it.*[10]

Does this mean that opposite-sex friendship is prohibited? No, it means that opposite-sex or third party *intimacy* is prohibited. Friendship and intimacy are not the same.

SIGNS OF CHANGE

Friendship as intimacy—particularly sexual intimacy—is showing signs of change. Today many Americans are among the "walking wounded." While looking for "meaningful opposite-sex relationships," they have been bushwhacked and robbed of their sense of self-worth and virtue. They feel angry and used by their so-called friends. One woman said:

> Four years ago everyone was giving lip service to having "meaningful relationships," but in the end they were in hot pursuit of "The Big O"—the ultimate orgasm. Giving and getting "good sex" (what is "good" anyway?) was the beginning and end of any decent companionship. . . . Going to bed on the first date was de rigueur. I remember how most of us felt that it was necessary to "get that out of the way" so that we could get on with the rest of the game plan. The only problem was that some of us never got beyond the opening act. Using sex as an ice-breaker became a dangerous substitute for dealing with a lot of nitty-gritty differences, . . . didn't bring automatic intimacy at all, nor did it even help a lot of us through the night.[11]

Having a date and *not* going to bed with him was a new and satisfying experience for this woman. Spending an evening sharing each other's "war stories" was more rewarding than sharing a bed. She said, "For some reason I find I value my relationships now. I want to be a long-distance runner and not a sprinter. Maybe it's a sign of age, but all I care about is making friends for life."[12] In the meantime, her girlfriend has gone through five devastating relationships that all started with instant, electric experiences at night and blown fuses in the morning.

This woman recalled her mother's secret of a successful thirty-seven-year marriage. Her mother had told her that sexual attraction wanes after a while. But she and her husband had become best friends, and more than that she truly respected him. Then the mother added, "What more could two people want?" That says it all. Sex can be found anywhere and at any time. But a good friend is hard to find.[13]

Another woman asks rhetorically, "Why can't a woman be friends with a man?" She responds that sexual tension is usually found in opposite-sex friendships—a tension that often leads to casual sex. But then she points out that "casual sex between friends only underscores our sexuality and reaffirms the difficulty of maintaining non-sexual friendships with men."[14]

She regrets that she can't be as unself-conscious and close to a man as she is with her female friends. But this kind of candor offers a bright future for opposite-sex friendships. We have enough history on Friendship American style to warn of the danger of friendship as intimacy, particularly in opposite-sex friendships. Women who write in women's magazines of their experiences are not sexually repressed Puritans who wouldn't know good sex even if it wore a name tag. They are women who are honest enough to admit that "a meaningful relationship" is too often a euphemism for "The Big O."

It looks like the day is dawning when we will return to some of the traditional values that have served us so well. One woman says, "Some say that there's a big return to conservatism. . .including Victorian romance. No wonder I've been enjoying the art form of dating so much. Last week I had my third date with this same fellow, and he took me to his reading group (everyone read from their favorite classical novels instead of reciting their latest neurosis) and, oh yes, we experienced our first kiss."[15]

CHAPTER FOUR
The Friendship Test

Our problem with understanding, defining, and enjoying friendship is due in large part to modern humanity's radical departure from the traditional idea of friendship as being appreciative-love, which had its focus on something outside of two friends. Friendship today is expressed more as need-love, and its focus is the people who meet our needs.

This does not mean that friends never notice each other. They do, but the bond they establish rises out of the struggle to achieve their vision—the thing that their friendship is about.

Friendship American style is a form of intimacy. Indeed, our dictionaries use the word synonymously. I look up the word *friend* and read that this is an "intimate associate." I look up the word *intimate* and read, "Closely acquainted or associated; very familiar (an intimate friend)."[1]

Let me propose three questions that can help us determine whether the relationship is friendship (appreciative-love), or intimacy (need-love).

I use the words *friends* and *intimates* to distinguish friendship from what it once was in the history of man and what it has become in modern times. I am not suggesting that having intimates is out of order. Indeed, intimate relationships can be quite proper, but they are workable only as long as both parties understand that there is a burden to intimacy that does not exist in friendship. Friends will help one another, but that is incidental to the friendship. Intimates *owe* it to help each other, because that is one of the burdens of intimacy. Don't let me need you and then not be there for me!

QUESTIONS TO ASK ABOUT FRIENDSHIP

On the basis of what I have already said in the previous chapters about friendship and intimacy, I propose three questions about friendship for the reader to ponder. Because the concern of this book is *opposite-sex* friendship, I will frame the questions accordingly—though the same may be asked about same-sex relationships.

WHAT IS THE FRIENDSHIP ABOUT? The first question to be asked has to do with the focus of the friendship. If a man and a woman say they are friends, we should ask what the friendship is about.

Friendship is about something other than each other.

Intimacy is about each other.

Lewis properly describes friends as having a shoulder-to-shoulder relationship, occupied with something outside of themselves. Intimates, on the other hand, behave much like lovers. They are face-to-face, occupied with each other. This does not mean that friends are not occupied with each other. But it is a mutuality they enjoy as a result of something *outside of themselves*—their common vision.

Married people have little problem when a spouse enjoys working with someone of the opposite sex who has the same vision. Whatever the two friends learn of each other is the result of their common vision—fighting side by side, arguing with each other, praying with each other. The bond established by this kind of relationship is quite different from that which a man and woman establish by looking into one another's eyes.

Sometimes people find this test of friendship difficult to understand because there seems to be nothing wrong with being personally interested in someone of the opposite sex so long as no immorality is involved.

Yet experience shows that many intimate opposite-sex relationships (both emotional and sexual) start out as friendships, particularly in the workplace. The focus of their relationship truly is outside of themselves. They work shoulder to shoulder, appreciating each other as teammates.

But if the two are attractive, and attractive to each other, they very easily slip into a face-to-face relationship. But because the slippage (initially) is so gradual and results in no immoral behavior, it often is ignored. What's wrong with looking forward to going to work with a co-worker who is attractive, personable, and makes you feel good? It's the old line that the moral relativism of the sixties popularized—how can it be wrong when it feels so good?

This condition ignored can lead to trouble. It is the wine connoisseur who, having merely appreciated the claret, now finds himself thinking about when he will have his next drink and planning to have it as soon as possible—without raising any questions about his growing need for the bottle. How many true friends have ruined their friendship because they, as the connoisseur, denied this growing and fatal attraction.

But what shall we say of the many single people whose single state does not inhibit such a turn of events, who may indeed be looking for more than friendship?

There is nothing wrong with friendship opening the way to emotional intimacy, as long as we acknowledge that this is what is happening and are willing to explore the burden of intimacy. As we shall see in chapter 7, singles run the risk of getting emotionally involved in a destructive game that seems to promise more than friendship but never commits to it.

IS IT APPRECIATIVE-LOVE OR NEED-LOVE? A second question to be asked deals with the nature of the love relationship. Friendship is properly called "love." But it is a different sort of love from that found in intimacy. This is true even in same-sex intimacy (see chapter 6).

Friendship appreciates the other person, but it doesn't need the other to survive.

Intimacy needs the other person for emotional survival.

I have pointed out earlier that the appreciative-love that friends feel for each other occurs in the context of what their friendship is about. Companions become friends, whether at play, at work, or in war, when they value the unique contribution of the other person to the activity.

Recently friends from out of state (a husband and wife) spent a month with my wife and me. They had stayed with us a couple of weeks the year before, but in the interim, we had contacted each other very little. But one thing I noticed about our friendship is that when we are together there's no sense of having to get acquainted all over. Yes, we may catch up on the news, but even then, the news is related in a way that is typically Bill and Audrey. We are concerned about what goes on in their lives. But their particular charm is not the details of their lives but how they talk about them.

I noticed the same in our activities, whether sightseeing, playing games, or boating. Their *way* of doing things and the way they looked at things was so totally in harmony with the way Fay (my wife) and I do and look at things, that it heightened the enjoyment.

They have been gone now for some time, and though we look forward to seeing them again next year, we haven't been in touch with each other. If they were to have a need that I could meet, I would fly at once to California to help them. But that is incidental to our friendship. We love them dearly as kindred spirits and enjoy them immensely when we're together. But we don't need them to survive nor do they need us.

Let me return to the claret connoisseur. When his claret is a thing of beauty and fine taste, something to be appreciated as an extra in life—not a requirement for survival—we have little worry about his fondness for it. But when appreciation turns to need, we worry.

The organization Al-Anon publishes a pamphlet (*Al-*

Anon: Is It for You?) for the family of the drinker to help them evaluate whether or not the person they love has a problem with alcohol and to determine if the family needs help from Al-Anon.

Instead of alcohol being our concern, let's reword their list a bit so we can use it to evaluate the opposite-sex relationship your husband or wife may be involved in:

1. You worry about how much he/she sees this other person.
2. You tell lies to cover up his/her relationship with this other person.
3. You feel that this other person is more important than you.
4. Meal times and activities are delayed because of his/her involvement with this other person.
5. You make threats to leave if he/she doesn't break off this relationship.
6. You kiss or make love to him/her to see if he/she is emotionally responsive or indifferent to you.
7. You're afraid to upset him/her because it may result in his/her seeking comfort from this other person.
8. You have been embarrassed by his/her behavior with this other person.
9. You have considered seeing a lawyer because you find your security threatened by his/her relationship with this other person.
10. You find yourself spying on him/her to confirm your suspicions about this relationship.
11. You have refused social invitations out of fear you'd be embarrassed by this relationship.
12. You sometimes feel guilty over the ways you have tried to intervene in this relationship.
13. You try to get him/her to break off the relationship by threatening to hurt yourself.
14. Others find you difficult to get along with because of your anger and preoccupation over this relationship.

Al-Anon has twenty items on its list, and they say that if three or more of them describe your situation, your loved one has an alcohol problem. I would say of my list that three out of fourteen would be a good test to help you determine whether your mate just appreciates or needs that other person.

I often hear the argument that marriage partners cannot give each other everything that is desired. I reply that it is within marriage that *needs* should be met. If physical and emotional survival *needs* are not being met in marriage, the couple should look diligently at their marriage to find out why.

If we're talking about appreciation or likes rather than needs, that's a different matter. Fay and I pursue some of our personal likes independently. We have many likes in common, but we have some we enjoy separately. It's important for an individual to enjoy his own company. But we seek fulfillment of our need for another person in each other and not in others. Is marriage and the family the place where we go for *needs* to be met? Is it the place we go *to survive*?

If you see nothing wrong with an opposite-sex friendship your mate is concerned about, ask yourself these questions:

1. Why do I really want this friendship?
2. How would I respond if my friend pressed for sex?
3. How threatened, upset, or uneasy would I be if my mate established an opposite-sex friendship?
4. Would I be bothered by what people say or think? Would I feel jealous, angry, or hurt if I or my friends saw my mate with another person?
5. How well do I deal with uncertainty? Would I still be able to maintain a loving relationship, knowing my partner is emotionally intimate with someone else?
6. Are the potential rewards of opposite-sex experimentation greater than the potential costs?[2]

Don't get bogged down in what *ought* to be. Remember that we're dealing with feelings. Rational arguments are fair game for debate; feelings never are. Maybe the feelings shouldn't be there. But they are. A loving relationship demands that feelings be respected and that solutions be generated with feelings in mind.

IS THE RELATIONSHIP INCLUSIVE OR EXCLUSIVE? A third question has to do with the inclusive or exclusive nature of the relationship.

Friendships happily include any and all who see things in the same way. Two is not the necessary number of friendship. This relationship is inclusive.

Intimacy happily excludes any and all. It does not wish to be disrupted by anyone else. This relationship is exclusive.

It is true that friends also are exclusive, but only in a group sense. It is the we against the them. The we would be very willing to admit to membership any and all who think in the same manner that they do. Indeed, it adds strength to the cause.

But intimates will not share. For an intimate to admit another person to the twosome raises the fear that his needs will not be met by the significant other.

This is what sibling rivalry is about. When two children are vying for Mom's attention she often asks, "Can't you two get along and be friends?" If the children understood the nature of the conflict they would tell her that they can't. They can't be friends and share the same mom because they have a need from their mom that no one else can fill. It is an intimacy that cannot be shared, for to do so would jeopardize one's own fulfillment of need.

When a "friend" becomes jealous of a third party who is admitted to the circle, it is doubtful that friendship existed between the original two. Intimacy and need-love, yes; but friendship, no. Friends share; intimates don't.

FRIENDSHIP AS THE MORE NOBLE LOVE

To some it may seem that I make friendship—appreciative love—a very "pale" love. I seem to portray friends as being less interested in one another than are intimates. And yet that's the very nature of appreciative-love and makes it more noble than need-love. C. S. Lewis says:

> In the Appreciative pleasures, even at their lowest, and more and more as they grow up into the full appreciation of all beauty, we get something that we can hardly help calling love and hardly help calling disinterested, towards the object itself.[3]

Parents who have difficulty letting go of their adult children don't understand disinterested love. Mothers sometimes tell me, "I can't let them go; I love them too much."

Their problem is that they don't love them enough, or more accurately, they love with an inferior love. They *need* their children. The children fill a space in their lives, which would be very empty if they left.

If they would truly love their adult children then let them love with the more noble love of appreciation. Let the children go to fulfill their God-given mission in life, and be glad to appreciate them from afar. Mother will then find gladness not from what her child does for her, but a gladness that this child with all his beauty, talent, and marvelous charm *exists* and is able to meet the needs of other human beings.

Shall we call this disinterested love as Lewis does? How, indeed, can a mother be *disinterested* in her child?

It is disinterested love in that the mother loves the child not for what she does for *him*, but for the fact that such a wonderful person as this should exist and that the world is the richer for his presence.

America has lost its sense of esthetics, its sense of what is truly beautiful quite apart from its functional value. And it probably is the reason why friendship has become need-love rather than appreciative love. Our fundamental sense of things is pragmatic. Of what *use* is it? Does it meet a *need*?

I can understand the insecurity of families in the Northwestern United States whose livelihood is jeopardized by environmentalists who seem to value ancient forests and the spotted owl more than people. The pragmatics of economic health make us wonder what price we are willing to pay for esthetics.

Yet what invaluable loss do we suffer when we sacrifice an appreciative-love for nature by trading it in for something that can be rung up on a cash register or reflected in the gross domestic product?

Our government is having a hard job sorting this out, mainly because of the difficulty we have calculating the benefits of appreciative-love. This brings me back to what I began with—the nobility of appreciative-love.

Intimacy may meet the need of starved souls. But friendship, with its appreciative, disinterested love, has the ability to enable our lives in a way that intimacy never could. We learn to value others not for what they can do for us, but simply because they exist.

CHAPTER FIVE

Successful Opposite-Sex Friendships

Men and women can be just friends if they thoroughly understand what friendship is. Friendship is *about* something besides each other. This is why a person's place of work is often where opposite-sex friendships develop. As we work, we discover like-minded people whom we grow to appreciate. That appreciation arises from the context of a common vision and goal.

WATCH YOUR BODY LANGUAGE

If opposite-sex friendship is to be successful, remaining in the realm of friendship, we must watch our body language. Body language is a behavioral pattern, an element of nonverbal communication.[1] An extremely popular subject in recent years, body language speaks volumes. People are beginning to realize that there is nothing mysterious about those who are popular with the opposite sex, never lacking dates. They are merely very articulate with their body language.

As evidence of its popularity, magazines carry advertisements offering to help readers become more adept at using body language. One full-page ad announces, HOW TO WIN AT LOVE! Below this heading is a picture of a man and woman, lips slightly parted, about to kiss. The ad offers "a simple up front way of telling someone you know you're attracted to them. . . ."[2]

My wife and I recently encountered a person very articulate in body language. We were just stepping onto a down-escalator in a shopping mall when a very attractive, well-dressed, well-groomed woman stepped onto the up-escalator coming in our direction. (I mention her appearance because it's important to the point I'm making.) The way in which she was dressed and groomed drew the attention of those around her. But that wasn't all. As she came toward us she gave me a momentary look that said volumes about what she was thinking. I was embarrassed and looked the other way. Fay was as miffed as I was embarrassed. When we stepped off the escalator Fay said disgustedly, "The nerve of her!"

My wife was quite right. "The nerve of her!" Not a word had been spoken, but all three of us knew what had been said. It was the unspoken language that goes on between men and women day in and day out. It was the body language that says, "I like what I see" or "I want you to know that I'm available."

We must aim to do the opposite of what books on body language suggest. We can learn to give the message that we're interested in something other than the sexual attractiveness of a person and that we're not available. Opposite-sex friendship is possible if we watch our body language and make it clear that we're interested in what the friendship is *about*. Appreciation of another person rises out of a common interest. In terms of body language, it is shoulder to shoulder rather than face-to-face.

To understand how to control body language, we need to understand people who don't. I am referring to people like the woman on the escalator, or to a man named Mike.[3]

Mike is a "lady's man." He knows how to come into a room full of people, spot an available woman, and single her out of the crowd. How does he do it? Ask a women, and she'll say, "I don't know. He just has his antennae out, I guess. I get signals, and I answer them, and the first thing I know. . . ."[4]

Mike's not a good-looking guy. But he has a sixth sense in regard to women. He knows how to let a woman know he's available. He also knows how to read signs from her as to her availability.

One woman, questioned about Mike, said, "I guess it's his aura." But on second thought she decided it was more definite than that. He dressed and groomed in such a way that he came across as a very attractive, masculine person. Even more attention-getting was the way he would stand and walk. A dozen little gestures emphasized a sexual message. In a room full of people Mike would lean against the mantel, glance around at the women, and then assume a posture with his legs apart and his hips thrust forward slightly as if they were cantilevered to his body. He would thrust his thumbs into his belt and point his fingers toward his genitals. His stance spelled *sex*.

One woman described Mike as having "easy grace." But a man who knew him was less kind. "Mike is greasy," he said. What may come through to a woman as being sexy is combative and distasteful to men.[5]

People who effectively send and receive signals find that it comes naturally. It begins with an attitude that says, "I think that I'm a sexy man (or woman). What do you think?" The man who is self-confident (rather than arrogant) converts that attitude into a language that effectively conveys confidence. This is body language, or psychocybernetics, at a practical level.

Body language might not be learned as easily as books on the subject promise because we must first believe in ourselves. Most people who try to use body language and fail have an attitude problem. They really don't have self-confidence, and they'd be shaken if they *did* get someone on the hook.

Attitude is a very important part of body language. If the confident attitude is there, it will come through in the body language. Several years ago I was chagrined by something a male acquaintance told me. I can't remember who he was or what the circumstances were. While talking with him about this subject I said that I was sometimes embarrassed by the behavior of women toward me—women who conveyed the message, "I like you. Let's get acquainted." He looked me straight in the eye and said, "Maybe the problem is *your* behavior, not theirs."

He was right. I pondered this for a long time and realized that I was sending the message to women, "Tell me that I'm an attractive man." When they would oblige, I found fault with *their* behavior.

Our body language reflects our attitude. What is it that we really want from the opposite sex? It's just as possible to convey the message, "I'm not interested in what you think of my attractiveness as a man or woman. I'm interested in our common goal, which is what this friendship is about," as it is to communicate, "Tell me I'm an attractive man (or woman)."

This is why it's important to see friendship as being *disinterested love*. A person may be attractive, but that's not where our interest lies. Friendship is about something besides the other person. Whether or not we have this attitude is obvious.

WHY THESE WOMEN ARE FRIENDS

As I look back over my adult life and think of my relationships with women, several stand out as friendships in the truest sense of the word. Though I mention just three, I can think of several others who are also good friends. I choose these three because our contact was in a close work environment, where most opposite-sex friendships occur.

JAN AND BONNIE. Even though I've seen Jan only once since I moved twenty years ago and haven't seen Bonnie in ten years, I still regard them both as friends.

Jan was my secretary for five years when I was a pastor in California. She is a very attractive woman, several years younger than I, is married, and has two children. My wife and I had some social contact with Jan and her husband, Bob, but most of my contact with Jan was at work.

Bonnie was my associate's secretary. Though I had less contact with her, everything I say about Jan applies also to her.

What distinguishes my friendships with both Jan and Bonnie is that neither ever expressed in body language anything that said, "Please notice me. Tell me that I'm an attractive woman." Nor did either send a message that said, "I want you to know you're an attractive man, and I like what I see." This was true of their dealings with me as well as with other men.

This does not mean that they were uncomfortable with their femininity, nor did they find me or other men unattractive. Male and female attractiveness was incidental to our relationships. We had something else in mind—our work or the social occasions we enjoyed with other friends.

Both Jan and Bonnie were warm and friendly, but they did two very important things. They established their territory, and they assumed a posture that clearly communicated that their minds were on the work at hand and not on whatever man might be present.

Dr. Edward T. Hall, professor of anthropology at Northwestern University, made a study of man's need to establish a territory and coined the word *proxemics* to describe his theory. He maintains that every human being has a need to establish a correct distance from other people, depending on the relationship. He sees four zones: (1) intimate distance, (2) personal distance, (3) social distance, and (4) public distance.[6] Different cultures have different rules for how much distance is appropriate for each zone. For example, Arab and Mediterranean men may hold hands, yet feel that there's still plenty of distance; there is no suggestion of unwholesome intimacy. By contrast, Americans are rather sensitive about touching. Jan and Bonnie established their territory and assumed a certain posture.

1. ESTABLISHING TERRITORY.

Dr. Hall says that there is a close phase and a far phase of personal distance—a range of two-and-one-half to four feet. When friends meet on the street and chat, they tend to stand at the far phase. The interpersonal message is that "we are friends, but social convention requires us to keep each other at arm's length."

This doesn't mean that a man and woman never touch. But what is the occasion? How is it done? I remember one occasion when, celebrating a particular triumph, I hugged Jan when she and her husband came into the room. But it was a cheek-to-cheek hug.

It is common to see opposite-sex hugging in mixed groups, but often it's full body hugging, hips to hips and chest to chest. This kind of "total" hugging may or may not be appropriate. We need to examine our motives. When we move from personal distance to intimate distance, what kind of message do we intend to send?

Dr. Leo Buscaglia—dubbed "Dr. Hug" by the press—will probably be listed in the *Guiness Book of World Records* as the man who has hugged and been hugged the most. A professor at the University of Southern California, he used to spend an hour or more after each of his lectures hugging up to a thousand fans.[7] Buscaglia sometimes makes love sound like a pragmatic feel-good technique benefiting the lover, but most of his prose is just a simple message of full-time kindness.[8]

Buscaglia began his kindness crusade in the late 1960s after a young female student committed suicide. Buscaglia says, "She was so beautiful and wonderful, and I thought, *What a tremendous loss of human potential.*"[9]

"Full-time kindness" is wonderful. But we must be honest about our motives. Are we just as inclined to hug the old, fat, and ugly as we are the young, well-proportioned, and beautiful? When we hug the young and beautiful, what do we have on our minds? Is it human kindness that we wish to impart? We cannot disguise our motive. It will be revealed in our behavior, and others will see it.

2. ASSUMING POSTURE. Jan and Bonnie not only established their territory, but also assumed a posture that sent an important message.

Dr. Albert E. Scheflen, professor of psychiatry at the Albert Einstein College of Medicine in New York City, says that men and women who want to send sexual messages will engage in "preening behavior." A woman may fluff her hair, check her makeup, or rearrange her clothes. A man may comb his hair, button his coat, or readjust his tie. When eye contact is made along with these gestures the body language is saying, "I'm interested. I like you. Notice me. I'm an attractive man (or woman)."[10]

Jan and Bonnie were always well-groomed, but I never saw "preening behavior." Neither seemed uncomfortable with their sexuality. They weren't Neoplatonists who couldn't have pure minds and be women too. Both were very feminine. But they established a territory and posture that made it clear that any intimate expression of their sexuality was reserved for their husbands.

CAROL. The other woman with whom I have had business dealings is Carol. She was director of author relations for a publishing house. My contacts with her always were while I was away from home on business trips. My wife has never met her, though she has spoken to her by phone.

The thing that distinguishes my friendship with Carol is that whenever we were together—driving in a car to appointments or having a meal together—the focus was on business and not on each other. Though the atmosphere was warm and cordial, she established a territory and a posture that were unmistakable. She is also attractive and comfortable with her sexuality and there is no message that says, "Do you find me attractive? I find you attractive." She does exactly what Jan and Bonnie did. She assumes a posture that says her mind is on business, not on the man she may be dealing with.

FRIENDLY FEEDBACK

Carol, Jan, and Bonnie confirmed my observations about our friendships. In interviews that included their husbands, I asked each of them the following questions:

IS IT REALLY FRIENDSHIP? My first question was, "Would you describe our relationship as friendship, which involves an appreciation for each other in a shoulder-to-shoulder effort where the focus is a common goal or interest rather than each other?" Each of them felt that described the relationship.

Carol pointed out that there was always a *reason* to be together. Our contacts were always about something other than each other. When we were together, she felt my respect for her and her talents. She remarked that the women editors felt the same respect. "They felt that you treated them as professional people rather than hirelings."

Jan expressed the same feeling. She felt that I appreciated her work and respected what she had to say. This gave her greater freedom to say what she thought about whatever we were working on and made her feel that she was an important part of the team effort.

Carol said, "I think at times the appreciation and respect came by way of asking for my input on something you were doing—asking my help at times. You showed that you understood what the lines of responsibility were within the company and came to me when it was appropriate."

Jan said that appreciation and respect were such important elements of the friendship, she became upset whenever anyone implied that our relationship was anything else. She said, "Sometimes people would come into the office and say, 'Well, have you been taking dictation on the pastor's knee?' What made me so angry was that it reflected on our friendship, and it was such a discredit to your character—demeaning!"

When Jan spoke of appreciation, I remembered how often I appreciated both Jan and Bonnie as bright, attractive, well-groomed, and well-spoken people, representing the office to the public. All these qualities enhanced the team effort.

COMFORTABLE BEHAVIOR AND ENVIRONMENT. The second question I asked was, "Did you find anything in my behavior or in our work or social environment that made you feel uncomfortable—that I had something in mind other than friendship?"

Jan and her husband, Bob, felt that a strong spiritual commitment and strong marriages helped to establish comfort. Jan felt that any questionable behavior would have been a great discredit to my character. The resulting loss of respect would have destroyed our friendship. She felt that because I didn't want to destroy friendship and a harmonious working relationship, she could count on my cultivating that respect.

Bob felt that a person cannot have a strong marriage and at the same time have a dalliance with someone else. From what he saw of my marriage, he felt it was strong. This made him feel comfortable about Jan's working with me.

Dave, Carol's husband, put it in terms of commitment. Friendship with a third party does not become intimacy when a husband and wife are committed to each other. He feels this commitment in his marriage and therefore feels secure. It's not a matter of sacrifice, however. He said, "I don't believe you can ever sacrifice for someone you love. You love them so much you desire what is best for them, and therefore there is no sacrifice."

Bonnie and her husband, Don, felt that our respect for each other's marriage helped define the limits of friendship. Anything that might have compromised the integrity of either marriage was simply out of the question. Yet this barrier to intimacy created a more comfortable friendship.

Don was away in Vietnam for much of the time Bonnie worked in the office. She felt free to call on me if she needed the assistance of a man. This affirms the fact that maintaining a proper distance in a relationship actually enhances friendship.

Carol feels that it's very easy to convey the message that she's a happily married woman by the way she conducts herself in business relationships. As a woman who travels a lot, there are some things she simply does not do. "I don't arrange a candlelight dinner for two." She always makes it clear that her purpose for being with the man is business. "I almost always carry a briefcase if I'm meeting a man at the airport or if I'm traveling or meeting someone for dinner," she said. This is a good example of a nonverbal message that says the purpose for being together is not each other.

Carol also said that she schedules appointments carefully. "I don't arrange anything late at night, and I make sure I'm where I'm supposed to be at what I feel is a proper time."

Without being specific about gender, she told of the experience of one friend, a salesperson, who has a client who tries to arrange meetings more frequently than necessary. "The account is being taken care of quite well, but [the client] wants to meet all the time with the sales rep, who happens to be quite attractive. On the surface it's all very innocent. It's under the guise of doing business. But the signals are there. For example, 'Let's meet for dinner at 6:00.' This is after the business day when there is no need for it. I suppose it could be rationalized, but taken as a package, it raises questions. A meeting after the business day, lingering over a meal too long when the business has been concluded—if there actually was any—just seems inappropriate." This is exactly what C. S. Lewis has in mind: What is the meeting *about*?

Bonnie agrees with Carol about the "signals" men send. She felt comfortable in our working relationship because there was none of that. She said, "I could never work in an environment very long under that kind of pressure. It's very true what you say about the way people look at each other— the kind of eye contact they maintain. A woman knows what a man is thinking by the way he looks at her. I had a bad experience in college. I had a project that required close contact with a faculty adviser. I was very glad when the project was done and I didn't have to see the man again. The look in his eyes told me that he had something on his mind other than the project."

THE IMPORTANCE OF OPENNESS AND PRIVACY. I asked Carol's husband, Dave, what it is about Carol that makes him feel secure with her being in the business world. He said it was their trusting relationship. "It's the openness we have with each other." He felt that Carol held nothing back of what was going on in her life. Their lives were open books to each other, but not to anyone else. Carol felt it proper to talk in general terms about one's spouse and family as it might indirectly relate to conversation with a friend. But she felt that sharing details violated the special bond she enjoyed with her husband. She affirmed the viewpoint of marriage counselors Leota and Robert Tucker that couples feel their relationship is special and that their close, private familiarity and warmth should not be compromised by opposite-sex intimacy.

I could sense the same quality in Don and Bonnie's marriage. They wrote each other every day while Don was in Vietnam and enjoyed a great deal of openness with each other. Don was ten thousand miles away, yet he knew more of what was going on in Bonnie's private life than I did, and I saw her every day. Because Bonnie knew that I respected her private life, she felt free to call on me if my help was ever needed. Proper boundaries actually created freedom in our friendship.

FRIENDSHIP AND FUN. Not all my contacts with Jan and Bonnie were strictly business. I asked them, "Did you ever feel in times of social contact, whether in or out of the office, that I violated the boundaries of friendship?"

Jan felt I had not crossed the boundaries. She especially valued social times as a way to draw together other kindred spirits—spouses included. She touched on the issue of two not being the necessary number for friendship. When we got together socially, it was a group function. We increased the enjoyment of our friendship by including others. What went on between us in the office was of interest to the others. All the husbands and wives in the group were private about what went on in their marriages. But the opposite was true about what went on among the friends in the group. The common commitment and vision, which we shared with each other, enriched the friendships.

OWNING OUR SEXUALITY

These friendships never carried a hint of sexual interest, so we never felt awkward because of the usual opposite-sex tension—you are woman and I am man. Because we believe that everything God created is good, including our sexuality, we looked very positively at the unique differences between men and women.

THE PSYCHOLOGY AND PHYSIOLOGY OF SEX DIFFERENCES. Men and women are different psychologically and physiologically.[11] One example of difference is male aggressiveness. Boys are both physically and verbally more aggressive in all cultures where behavior has been studied. Mock fighting and fantasies are indirect forms of their aggression, and they also display direct forms of aggression more frequently than do girls. Aggressive behavior is found as early as social play begins—around age two. The aggressiveness of both sexes declines with age, but males remain more aggressive through college years. The victims of male aggression are usually other males.

The sex difference in aggression cannot be blamed on socialization, though society reinforces it. Male aggression has a biological foundation.

Male hormones (androgens) function during prenatal development to masculinize the growing individual. Females who are exposed to abnormally high levels of androgens prenatally are masculinized both physically and behaviorally.

Experiments with rodents show that giving testosterone to infant female rodents increases fighting in adulthood. By contrast, giving the female hormone, estrogen, reduces adult fighting. [12]

There are also physiological differences between male and female. Woman's basal metabolism is lower than man's. The sexes differ in skeletal structure—woman having a shorter head, broader face, less protruding chin, shorter legs, and longer trunk. Boys' baby teeth last longer than do girls'. A woman has a larger stomach, kidneys, liver, and appendix, but smaller lungs. Her vital capacity or breathing power is lower. Her blood contains more water and 20 percent fewer red cells. Since these supply oxygen to the body cells, she tires more easily and is inclined to faint. The blood cells affect the short-term viability of women. When the workday in British factories was increased from ten to twelve hours under wartime conditions, the number of accidents involving women increased 150 percent; the number of accidents involving men remained the same.

Men have 50 percent more brute strength than do women. Women have several important uniquely female functions— menstruation, pregnancy, and lactation. All these factors influence behavior and feelings. A woman has more and different hormones than a man does. A gland common to both sexes behaves one way in a woman and in a different way in a man. Thus a woman's thyroid is larger and more active; it enlarges during pregnancy and menstruation; it makes her prone to goiter, provides resistance to the cold, and is associated with three important elements of personal beauty—smooth skin, a relatively hairless body, and a thin layer of subcutaneous fat. The thyroid also contributes to more pronounced emotional ups and downs—a woman laughs and cries more easily than does a man.[13]

These differences mean that man and woman behave and interact differently. In relationships these differences can complement each other. But this cannot happen if either man or woman represses sexuality or acts as though it is insignificant, meaningless, or suited only for recreational activity in bed.

We must own our sexuality and permit the psychology and physiology of male-female differences to enrich our opposite-sex friendships. Woman can learn much from the native aggression of man. Man can learn much from the social skills woman uses to avoid confrontation and the finesse with which she works her way out of an awkward situation.

We owe it to each other not to reduce our sexuality to mere recreation. As friends we need to be fully functional as men and women in a complementary manner.

FRIENDSHIP IS UNINQUISITIVE. My friendships with Jan, Bonnie, and Carol are complementary. All three respect me. I feel appreciative-love from them—they feel my respect and appreciative-love in return.

The quality of "uninquisitiveness" is what makes these friendships work. Anything personal we learned about each other came in a roundabout way. For example, "I am angry because. . ." or "I am late because. . . ," followed by a personal explanation.

The primary focus of our relationship is our work and not each other. C. S. Lewis puts it this way:

> *Friendship, unlike Eros, is uninquisitive. You become a man's Friend without knowing or caring whether he is married or single or how he earns his living. What have all these "unconcerning things,*

matters of fact" to do with the real question, Do you see the same truth? In a circle of Friends each man is simply what he is: stands for nothing but himself. No one cares twopence about anyone else's family, profession, class, income, race, or previous history. Of course you will get to know about most of these in the end. But casually. They will come out bit by bit, to furnish an illustration or an analogy, to serve as pegs for an anecdote; never for their own sake. This is the kingliness of Friendship. We move like sovereign princes of independent states, abroad, on neutral ground, freed from our contexts. This love (essentially) ignores not only our physical bodies but that whole embodiment which consists of our family, job, past, and connections. At home, besides being Peter or Jane, we also bear a general character; husband or wife, brother or sister, chief, colleague or subordinate. Not among our Friends. It is an affair of disentangled, or stripped, minds. Eros will have naked bodies; Friendship naked personalities.[14]

Jan and Bonnie know my family, and we theirs—but not by prying into each other's personal lives. It was our respect for each other's marriage and its integrity that provided a natural barrier to inquisitiveness. The attitude was, "You have your marriage; I have mine. This is a part of your life that is your own private business and really has nothing to do with the truth that occupies us as friends."

This is far from Neoplatonism. We don't hide our sexuality or remove it from our minds or personalities. Sex, as being either male or female, is present in the way we look at life and in the way we formulate ideas. This is possible because sex as far as what we do is reserved for marriage. Our friendships work because they are uninquisitive.

WHAT TO DO WHEN THERE IS SEXUAL TENSION. Sexual tension results when two people find each other sexually attractive. But that tension doesn't make friendship impossible. It can be turned into a wholesome experience.

We have a valuable analogy to opposite-sex relations

within the family, particularly father–daughter relations where incest is a grave possibility.

It is natural for a son to develop romantic feelings for his mother and a daughter for her father. It is common for a daughter to test her sexual prowess on her father by behaving coquettishly. A father, alarmed by his own sexual feelings, may make the mistake of becoming angry or cold. He may even ridicule his daughter's behavior. This turns a normal situation bad. She may accept the message that she is a loser as a female, withdraw, and become sexually stunted and inhibited; or she may increase her flirtatious behavior and become promiscuous with boys and men in an effort to be told, "You're a winner as a woman."

A wise father does not tell his daughter about his feelings, though it will be evident by his behavior that he recognizes she is a potent female. His words and actions must say, "Honey, you're not a little girl anymore. You're a very attractive woman. I'd appreciate it if you'd wear more clothes around the house" or "I'd appreciate it if you didn't touch me like that." By his words and behavior the father says two things: first, his daughter is an attractive, potent woman; and second, a proper father–daughter relationship requires that they avoid sexually stimulating words and behavior. By this response, the daughter's femininity is affirmed and proper sexual decorum is taught. The daughter is then much less likely to be sexually promiscuous.

Counselors face the same task with opposite-sex clients. They can affirm a client's sexual potency without any immoral or unethical behavior. The issue is this: *Because* you are a sexually potent person, proper safeguards must be exercised.

What is required in the family and in a counseling setting is exactly what is required in opposite-sex friendship. Because a friend is sexually potent and because we respect him (or her) and wish only the best for him, we behave in a manner that shows respect and true selfless love. This is true friendship.

CHAPTER SIX
Alternatives to Opposite-Sex Friendships

Opportunities for opposite-sex friendship should not distract us from other friendships. Friendship with ourselves, with members of the same sex, and with couples are rewarding friendship possibilities.

BE YOUR OWN FRIEND

The greatest untapped opportunity for friendship lies within ourselves. If we would develop those qualities that make a person a good friend, we would find our own company enjoyable. Then we'd never be without a friend.

Fay and I like to spend long summer weekends at the oceanfront—just the two of us. Sometimes we are together talking, people-watching, or playing backgammon. At other times she reads while I surf or take long walks on the beach.

As we were heading home after one summer weekend, I told her that I had had a great time with my two best friends—my wife and myself. The togetherness we had shared and my time spent alone combined to make it a wonderful weekend.

THE IMPORTANCE OF INDIVIDUALITY. For friendship to exist, people must be individuals. The equation of togetherness in marriage is not 1 + 1 = 1. It is 1 + 1 = 3. Two individuals together make a third entity—a couple. It might be diagramed this way:

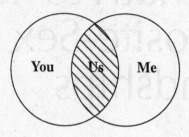

Figure 5

There can't be an "us" without a "you" and a "me." The vitality of the "us" depends on the vitality of the individuals who make up "us." Many marriages suffer a lack of friendship because the husbands and wives don't develop their individuality and therefore have nothing to bring into the us part of the relationship. One of the cruelest things I've ever seen a husband do to his wife is keep her so busy being a wife and mother that she never develops as a person—then he has an affair with someone who is more interesting! The other woman is probably more interesting because she has blossomed as an individual.

THE UNDEVELOPED INDIVIDUAL. There are several reasons why married people, particularly wives, don't become individuals.

1. Sometimes it's owing to self-hate. We can't be friends with ourselves if we don't like ourselves. This is often the result of a poor self-image developed during childhood.

My mother was an excellent role model of a person who liked herself. She not only liked herself, but she was comfortable about saying so. She was a semi-professional singer, performing in churches and synagogues. I remember my dad's asking her how she did after singing at a high holy days service in a synagogue. She replied with a broad grin, "I was great!" She was, and there was nothing arrogant about her statement.

A healthy self-image is important. Parents who demonstrate that they know when they have done well and when they have not done well are examples for their children to follow. Children often reflect in significant ways the self-image of one or both of their parents.

2. Sometimes we don't cultivate our individuality because we are dominated by a possessive spouse. The wife, more frequently than the husband, remains undeveloped for this reason. Her role as wife and mother is all the possessive husband cares about. Any sign of her functioning as an individual apart from these roles is met with everything from petulance to anger.

I have seen marriages ruined by men who view marriage as $1 + 1 = 1$. The man may have no interests of his own and smothers his wife or applies a double standard—he has his individuality, but will not permit her the same.

I will deal more extensively with possessiveness in chapter 9, but this much must be said here: This kind of man really doesn't want his wife as a friend. He may say he does. His wife though must be an individual and enjoy peer status in order to be his friend. What the possessive husband really wants is a cook, a maid, and a laundress who is also his lover.

3. Another reason why we fail to develop ourselves and have good self-images is that we subscribe to a false Christian ethic. We misunderstand what it means to "love your neighbor as yourself." This kind of love presupposes a healthy self-love. But many of us act as though we should love our neighbor *instead of* ourselves.

The apostle Paul urges Christians to "honor one another above yourselves" (Rom. 12:10 NIV). We are able to put others first because we are in the habit of meeting our own needs and taking care of ourselves. We can give to others only out of our own fullness.

The person with a false ethic often becomes manipulative. He cannot meet his own needs or even ask that they be met. He may intimidate others into meeting his needs by means of anger or by using petulance to make them feel guilty.

HOW TO BE YOUR OWN FRIEND. Being your own friend is an art that can be learned. Nina is a good example of this truth.

I met Nina several years ago when she came for counseling. She had been suffering from agoraphobia for many years. She was afraid of going places alone. She was terrified to drive to the supermarket, and if she did, the idea of standing in line panicked her. She even found it difficult to go into some rooms of her home by herself.

Nina fit the classic phobic pattern. She had a poor self-image, and her phobia was most likely a spontaneous, uncontrollable cry for help. She felt sure this was the case. She added that she had never felt loved or accepted by her husband, Clyde. "If only I were smarter, prettier, or better organized, then he would love me," she said. "Clyde thought I wanted him to 'fix' everything and solve my problems, but he said he was at a loss to know what to do. *I* didn't want him to *fix* anything. All I wanted was for him to hold me, tell me he was there, and say that I would get through this stronger than ever for it. But it never happened."

Nina eventually faced the reality that Clyde wasn't going to give her the kind of relationship she wanted. She had to develop her own security and self-image. Week after week I encouraged her to get on with her own life and become an individual in her own right. She didn't have to divorce Clyde or even separate from him. But she did have to become an individual.

One day she came into the office beaming. I knew something had happened. It turned out that she had been thinking about this business of being an individual when it had finally clicked.

She said, "I realized that when I got married I had stopped being myself. I was living in someone else's shadow. Clyde's ideas had become my assignments. His future and career had become my purpose for existence. His choices had become my choices. When I realized this, I decided that I'd start, in small ways, to do things my way. I didn't make things miserable for him, but I dared not to do everything his way. For example, when I bought pickles, instead of getting dill because that's what Clyde likes, I got sweet *because that's what I like*. I made decisions about my work without consulting him. If I wanted to work at home when he wanted to go to the farm, I did. And he went by himself."

Not only had Nina learned to be an individual, but in doing so she finally laid to rest her agoraphobia. She no longer needed to cry for help. She said, "Now I'm beginning to understand what it means to be your own friend. The other person I was looking for was *me!* There she was—a person who knows me better than anyone else. Someone who always would be there, understanding, caring, encouraging me, loving me. I wasn't going to explain myself anymore or justify who I am. How beautiful! What inexpressible joy not to need someone else to be there to agree with me before I believe it. How could I have overlooked this friend?"

SAME-SEX MALE FRIENDS

Alfred, Lord Tennyson wrote,

> 'Tis better to have loved and lost
> Than never to have loved at all.

These lines are often quoted when a man and woman part. Few people are aware that this verse was written to celebrate the love of one man for another.

Tennyson penned these words in his masterpiece, *In*

Memoriam. In this part of the elegy he laments the death of his dear friend, Arthur Henry Hallam, who died in Vienna on September 15, 1883. The poem is quite remarkable (at least to modern man) for the unself-conscious manner in which Tennyson writes of his love for another man. Now that Hallam is dead, Tennyson feels a "vaster passion" that comes diffused through God and nature, and he writes about it in his elegy.[1]

For men to use the word "passion" to describe their friendships in Tennyson's day and in earlier times was not unusual. The public's sexual sensitivities were not bombarded in the nineteenth century as they have been during the past forty years in the Western world. The word "passion" was not synonymous with sex. It was a noble emotion. The agony and triumph of Christ, for example, are spoken of as "the Passion of Christ." It's a red-blooded emotion that had nothing to do with sexual feeling.

A little earlier in the same century, Emerson wrote of same-sex friends in a similar vein:

> *A ruddy drop of manly blood*
> *The surging sea outweighs;*
> *The world uncertain comes and goes,*
> *The lover rooted stays.*[2]

There is not a hint of self-consciousness as Emerson writes of this "lover." Homosexuality was not suggested, because "friendship" was not a euphemism for sexual relations.

C. S. Lewis says,

> *Kisses, tears and embraces are not in themselves evidence of homosexuality. The implications would be, if nothing else, too comic. Hrothgar embracing Beowulf, Johnson embracing Boswell (a pretty flagrantly heterosexual pair), and all those hairy old toughs of centurions in Tacitus, clinging to one another and begging for last kisses when the legion was broken up . . . all pansies? If you can believe that you can believe anything. On a broad historical view it is, of course, not the demonstrative gestures of Friendship among our*

ancestors but the absence of such gestures in our own society that calls for some special explanation. We, not they, are out of step.[3]

This absence of such gestures is the legacy of our sexually sensitized era—a loss of passion for anything except sex. It seems that for the past forty years we have been so preoccupied with sex that our senses have been dulled. We can no longer see two men or two women loving each other nonsexually with appreciative-love—even appreciative-love that could be called passion.

That is not to say that appreciative-love relationships are free from complications. Such friendships have dangers, particularly for people with weak gender identity. These people need to be as brutally honest about their friendships as does the person with strong gender identity. Because close human relationships today are almost always suspected of being of sexual interest, men are afraid to get close to each other. What boy has not grown up fearing the label "fag"? So he relates to his male buddies in a way that could not be construed as love—not even appreciative-love.

When men hug each other they use a protocol to assure themselves and anyone watching that there's nothing there that might be construed as being sexual love—they slap each other's backs. It is sad that society has dictated that male friendship be little more than backslaps and six-packs.

ATTITUDES TOWARD MALE FRIENDSHIPS. Ten years ago a survey inquired into what men thought of friendship with other men. Surprisingly, the majority didn't think male-male friendships were possible—mainly because friendship in America was evolving into something American males were not prepared for—intimacy, affection, and sensitivity. The American male shied away from these behaviors because they were foreign to the role he had been raised to fill.[4]

Over the past ten years men's attitudes have begun to

change. Steve Largent, the NFL's all-time pass receiver, says,

> Men have very few friends whom they feel they can reveal everything to. A lot of men don't have anybody—not even their wives—with whom they feel comfortable enough to talk. By developing relationships with other men, they can open up and express themselves freely.[5]

This change of attitude has contributed to the growth of a Christian men's movement, of which such ministries as Career Impact, Priority Living, Christian Business Men's Committee, and AbbaFather are a part.

The Rev. Gordon Dalbey, author of *Healing the Masculine Soul* says that men are caught between a women's movement that requires that they abdicate masculinity to gain sensitivity and Rambo-like media portrayals of manhood. He says that Jesus Christ must be our model of manhood.[6]

One trend among men's groups is the "accountability group" in which they ask questions of each other such as, "How is it *really* going with your wife," and "How are you spending your free time?" Men seem to be less inhibited answering to other men then they are to their wives. Single men also find the groups helpful in developing sensitivity and intimacy.[7]

Many Christian wives are delighted to see their husbands involved in groups like these. The men are learning to become open and vulnerable to other men and are willing to be accountable. But some wives voice concern.

"When my husband, Don, first got involved with his accountability group I thought it was great," Laura told me. "I thought this openness and vulnerability would translate into a stronger commitment to church and home.

"Don has been in this group for several years now, but none of his activity has resulted in a warmer, more intimate, or more communicative relationship *with me*. In fact I'm becoming jealous of his male friends. They have an intimacy with him that *I* don't have!"

FRIENDS OR INTIMATES? Laura raises a legitimate concern and caution. The Christian men's movement today runs the risk of tampering with the intimacy of the husband–wife relationship.

First of all, as Laura complained, married men are able to get closer to each other, but this doesn't always translate into a stronger marriage. I have no problem with *single men* developing emotional intimacy with each other, so long as they are willing to accept the burden of intimacy and fulfill their responsibilities to each other. What is more, having learned to develop intimacy, they are in a position to be intimate with their wives if they marry. But with married men, emotional intimacy with other men can rob marriage of this needed dynamic. Men may have sexual intimacy with their wives, but without emotional intimacy, it's not complete.

I tackled Laura's problem by suggesting that the four men from her husband's accountability group get together with their wives for a couples' group. They agreed, and when it was all over, they were pleased with the results.

Laura's husband was able to tell her that he found it easier to talk with his men friends than with her. He said that whenever he told her something she didn't like she either verbally attacked him or behaved in a manner that nonverbally communicated her displeasure just as effectively.

"I just don't want to get into any substantive discussions with you," Don said. "I keep everything superficial—and safe."

In the group we were able to monitor Laura's style of communicating with Don and help her see the many ways in which *she* was standing in the way of intimacy with him. She didn't like what she heard and often became angry and defensive with the group. But we didn't let her off the hook until she accepted some responsibility for inhibiting Don's openness. Don was also able to see that he had a responsibility not to retreat into silence whenever Laura confronted him.

Don discovered that it was easier to communicate with his men's group than with the couples' group where his wife was present. If the men didn't like something, and said so, he could walk away and go home. With his wife, it was another matter. Their physical, financial, emotional, and spiritual lives were so intertwined as to make the cost of miscommunication and failed intimacy very high. Rather than discouraging him, this revelation made Don willing to do the hard work of developing intimacy with his wife rather than with other men.

Good things happened to the other couples too. The results were so rewarding that the men dissolved their group and the four couples established a *couples'* accountability group.

A second concern I have about men's groups is that by failing to identify the true nature of their relationship— calling it friendship when it's intimacy—they make married men vulnerable to dangerous opposite-sex relationships.

What if a married man in a men's group learns to be warm and vulnerable, communicative and intimate, and decides to cultivate this kind of a "friendship" with a woman at work? What would the men's group say? What would his wife say? What would the other woman's husband say? All of a sudden the social skills the man has learned to express so well in his male group of "friends" are now subject to scrutiny and suspicion.

What has happened? Is there a difference between friendship with another man and friendship with a woman? No! True friendship in both cases is appreciative-love, not need-love. And that's why men and women can be friends. But it's dangerous to have opposite-sex friends when nobody is quite clear as to what friendship is!

A major reason why men and women have difficulty being friends in our society is that we muddle the distinction between appreciative-love and need-love. As long as two people are in a same-sex relationship it doesn't seem to matter whether we call it friendship or intimacy—except in cases like that of Laura, who feels left out. But when *the very same* social interplay occurs between a married person and someone of the opposite sex outside of marriage we begin to get nervous—and properly so!

We must maintain the distinction between friendship and intimacy in all relationships, whether it be with the same or opposite sex. By doing so we have a consistent standard by which we can evaluate relationships and make it possible for men and women to be just friends.

SAME-SEX FEMALE FRIENDS

Women are at greater risk of establishing an intimate relationship and calling it friendship than are men because they develop intimacy much more readily than do men.

While boys are taught to compete, girls are taught to be sensitive, to be people oriented, and to be socially aware. This helps girls during adolescence when boys' physical development gives them a competitive edge in sports. Girls learn to compete in other ways. By becoming socially aware and adept in people relationships girls find that they don't need physical strength to compete effectively with emerging men. They simply outmaneuver them with their social skills, which the men probably won't learn until their middle years when their strength begins to wane.

Because it's "okay" for women to be sensitive, feeling, and emotional, *they fit easily into the modern idea of friendship as being intimacy*. Most women find it easy to talk about their innermost feelings. Because they develop social skills earlier than men—skills that include recognizing their feelings and talking about them—they are better at relating to other women on an intimate level.

Same-sex friendship can be valuable and rewarding, but caution must be exercised. When a so-called friendship really is same-sex emotional intimacy, it can adversely affect career and marriage.

FRIENDSHIP AT THE OFFICE. Women often like to have one special friend at the office—a woman they can tell their personal and professional troubles to and share their triumphs with as well. But such friendships rarely work on the job for long, and the reason is that *they are not friendships*. Even though the person may be called a "best friend," the relationship is *emotional intimacy*.

"Forming a close, mutual support, let-your-hair-down relationship with another woman in your office is a potentially dangerous situation," warns career counselor Janice LaRouche. "It can be as dangerous as having an affair with a male colleague."[8]

This intimacy, which LaRouche calls a best-friend relationship, may go well at the junior level, but what happens when there's a promotion? A boss cannot be boss and maintain an intimate relationship with someone who works for her. Certain favors may be expected of the newly promoted boss; when the favors are not granted, the disappointed intimate may become vindictive.

Whether the intimacy is sexual as in the case of an opposite-sex affair or emotional as in this case, the same problem surfaces. We feel that intimates owe us things that friends do not.

At work primary loyalty is to the job, not to co-workers. Management knows this and views with suspicion any relationships that are too thick and may work against the interest of the company.

Certain dos and don'ts ought to be observed in the office:

- *If you're starting a job, DON'T team up right away with the first person who makes friendly overtures. There's often a reason why that person is anxious to get acquainted with the newcomer—she may have alienated everyone else. Furthermore, she may be looking for something more than friendship. She may have unfulfilled needs that she expects you to fill.*

- *DO keep your distance for a·while. Be friendly with everyone, but don't commit yourself to one person or one group too soon.*

Your aim is not to have one "best" friend, or intimate. It is to develop many friendships (appreciative-love relationships).

- *If a superior is overly anxious to get close to you, DO beware. An invitation to socialize after work is flattering, and you may suppose that it's a good way to get to know each other, but if it's just the two of you, it's more than friendship. She may be seeking an emotional intimacy, which though not morally wrong, may not be good for your career because others will say that you have something special going with the boss. If the socializing is done as a group, that's another matter.*

- *If you're the boss, counsel and guide your assistant, but DON'T make a pal of her. Take her to lunch on her birthday, but find lunch companions on your own managerial level. Friendship and emotional intimacy work on the same grade level but not above or below.*

- *If a friend gets promoted, DON'T resent it. If she's really your friend, you'll be glad for her—and meanwhile try to catch up by doing better yourself.[9]*

FRIENDSHIP AMONG HOMEMAKERS.

Friendship opportunities present themselves at home as well as at the office. Having friends besides your husband will not jeopardize your marriage, so long as it is true friendship—appreciative love, not need-love.

Problems arise when the wife establishes an emotional intimacy with another woman, tells her about the troubles in her marriage, relies on her for emotional support, and fails to deal with her lack of emotional intimacy with her husband. Though there's nothing morally wrong with such a relationship, it keeps the husband–wife relationship from developing the kind of emotional intimacy it should have.

If a woman's husband has made it clear that he does not wish to fill his wife's need for emotional intimacy, then she may need to seek it elsewhere, but certainly not with another man! Other women are safer candidates for intimacy in a case like this.

In seeking an intimate, the married woman must keep in mind the difference between friends and intimates. Friends may meet each other's needs, but meeting needs is incidental to friendship. Intimacy, on the other hand, focuses on need and is willing to accept the burden that goes with it. In chapter 3 I discussed the burden of intimacy. Remember, if you let me need you, then you must be ready to be there for me.

I do not object to people developing intimacies outside of their family of origin or their marriage. What I object to is calling those intimacies "friendship." Our failure to distinguish between friendship and intimacy has been an unending source of confusion and hurt in human relationships.

Having said that, let me offer some cautions.

First, the married woman must be careful that she doesn't use her female intimate as a marriage counselor. Nonprofessionals are not likely to be as objective as professionals or have the training necessary to understand the complexities of marital discord.

Second, if you are ever sought out to fill the role of an emotional intimate, watch out for the "bottomless-pit." Often a younger woman looking for an intimate will flatter an older woman with attention and favors and then become neurotically demanding of her time. The bottomless-pit doesn't really want to solve her problems. In fact, she *needs* her problems to give her an excuse to relate to you. If you would help her, don't indulge her. If she really wants help she will find a doctor or professional therapist who can help solve her problems or confront her with the fact that she really doesn't want to solve them. Intimates are not professional problem solvers.

DEVELOPING SAME-SEX FRIENDSHIPS

Here are some dos you should pay attention to in cultivating same-sex relationships:

- *DO remember that friendship is about something, and that it's appreciative-love. Problems can be avoided by reserving intimacy for spouse or family, or if you're single, for that person who is willing to explore (with a view to marriage) a relationship that involves not only friendship but also intimacy.*

- *DO remember that friends are not made, they are discovered. We must be involved socially if we would have friends. Scour the newspaper for activities that may be of interest. Many newspapers publish a calendar of local activities and events—a rich source of information telling where like-minded people might be found. Church bulletins, chambers of commerce, and publications of service organizations such as the Rotary Club, Kiwanis, and the Lions offer information about activities that may be of interest.*

- *DO dare to do something different. Perhaps you've never joined a hiking club, a bowling league, or a camera club. Try one. If it's a bore, move on to something else. Be brave. Explore.*

- *DO beware of exclusivity in friendship. Remember that friendship is inclusive. "Best friends" sometimes turn out to be needy people seeking emotional intimacy.*

- *If you're married, make sure your spouse is your friend. If you're single and have discovered no suitable friend or your spouse doesn't care to be your friend, consider being your own friend.*

COUPLE FRIENDSHIPS

Susan and Joanna had been friends since college, but they have seldom had a chance to see each other alone since Joanna's marriage five years ago. Susan's husband always wanted to make a "foursome" of social occasions. But Susan resented this intrusion. She felt that it interfered with her friendship with Joanna, so Susan and Joanna settled for intimate phone conversations instead of face-to-face encounters. But Susan sadly concluded, "Something precious has gone out of our relationship."[10]

Josh, another of Susan's friends, is a newspaper reporter. He married a tax lawyer who never liked his newspaper friends in general and Susan in particular. Susan and Josh see each other anyway when one of them makes a business trip to the other's town. They go out to lunch or dinner, but Josh lies to avoid a fight. It bothers both of them that Josh lies. "But," Susan says, "it doesn't bother me enough to end a twelve-year friendship or to sit through dreary three-way meals in which the pleasure of two friends is destroyed by the boredom and antipathy of a third person."

Susan contends that the problems with her two friendships are not a lack of time for meeting or a jealous wife. She contends that they are rooted in the same problem, which she calls "the Great American Couple Friendship Fiction."[11]

IS COUPLE FRIENDSHIP A FICTION? Susan thinks that couple friendship is fiction for a number of reasons. She maintains that couples have a strange idea about what it means "to become one" when they marry. She asserts that there's no law that says a husband and wife are going to like each other's friends. "In adopting 'togetherness' as a social standard," she says, "Americans reacted to social segregation that was practiced by many of their immigrant parents and grandparents. The trouble is that we substituted compulsory coupledom for compulsory separation of the sexes."[12] She laments that it is almost impossible for anyone who makes up one-half of a pair to sustain a serious individual friendship with an outsider of either sex.

There are two main reasons why many couples don't like friendships that exclude one of the spouses.

One reason, particularly in opposite-sex friendship, is suspicion. The threat of infidelity always looms. If not physical infidelity, they fear what, in the past, was called "alienation of affection." Affection for the friend may preempt affection for the spouse.

Another reason, less clear and bordering on possessiveness, is simply being displaced by another person. One man said, "It's like a slap in the face to me if my wife chooses to go out for the evening with a woman friend instead of with me. It's as if she is saying, 'I'll enjoy what I'm doing tonight more with someone else than with you.' "[13]

Couples usually reserve after–dinner hours during the week and weekends for themselves, even though they may not be doing anything together. One may watch television while the other pursues a different activity somewhere else in the house or yard. Yet they seem to sense that they are fulfilling their need for togetherness. The relationship is often strained when one or the other says, "Since we're not doing anything, I think I'll go out with my friends."

We must look carefully at the idea of togetherness in marriage. Possessiveness is wrong and can be damaging, but there is some justification for spouses' feeling displaced.

THE PRIMARY FRIENDSHIP. An essential feature of an enduring marriage is primary friendship with each other. When a man and woman fall in love, they become totally occupied with one another. Other friendships don't hold the same attraction. The couple are in love. Most friends understand this. But being in love seems to be a condition that most people get over. When this happens, couples tend to resume previous lifestyles.

There's nothing wrong with being in love. But the years ahead are sustained and maintained by friendship and other qualities of love. That is why, if the marriage is to endure, a couple must develop their personal friendship as being the primary friendship—making each other best friends. Chapter 8 will deal with this further.

When romance begins to fade and the couple, as individuals, begin to return to old friendships instead of developing friendship with each other, the marriage is deprived of a necessary element. Primary friendship with each other means that other friendships are subordinate.

Many marriages fail because friendship with each other doesn't exist. So partners fulfill their friendship desires outside the marriage, robbing themselves of the very thing they need to survive as a couple.

A certain amount of resentment is justified, therefore, when a husband or wife says, "Yes, I would rather be with someone other than you." It raises the question, "Is there something wrong with *our* friendship?" Too often the answer, though unspoken, is, "Yes. You have been a great lover for the past year—or fifteen years. But a friend you're not." What is worse, they are unwilling to talk about the lack of friendship in their relationship. It may reveal an ugly truth: "I think you're a sexy person, but I really don't like you. Most of the time you're really not comfortable to be around."

If friends tolerate our preoccupation with our spouses when we're in love, why shouldn't they tolerate our preoccupation with our spouses as friends? True togetherness does not mean the loss of individuality. The equation of a successful marriage, as we saw earlier in the chapter, is $1 + 1 = 3$. Two individuals are also a couple. When they function effectively, they enrich the coupling relationship.

Fay and I are very different. She is retiring, quiet, friendly, sensitive, kind, and modest about her abilities. She shuns disagreements, does not force her opinions on others, and would rather follow than lead. I am all of the opposite. My friendship with her has introduced me to an entirely different way of looking at life and relating to people. She has enriched me as a person and has helped me see ways in which I can be much more effective in my relations with others. I am far more interested in what Fay's friendship has to offer than I am in any other friendship. I don't feel a loss by putting her friendship first. Should I feel the desire to cultivate other friendships, I need to ask the question, "Does this imply a lack in my primary friendship?" If it doesn't, and if other friendships don't take anything away from my friendship with Fay, fine.

TWO COUPLES CAN BE FOUR FRIENDS IF . . . If a husband and wife truly are friends, it's very likely that they will be friends with another couple. Consider this: If A and B are friends and C and D are friends, then it follows that if A and C are friends, it's likely that B and D will also be friends. The common bond that any two of them experience will most likely be experienced by all four. The great weakness with couple friendships is that *husbands and wives are not their own best friends*. There can be no common bond among A, B, C, and D because there is none between A and B or C and D.

Dale and Frankie Lou are a good example of a great couple friendship. Dale was my associate when I was a pastor in California. The four of us have always been close, working together and playing together. We owned a sailboat together for a time. The only reason we don't enjoy each other now is that we live five hundred miles apart. Fay and I look forward to their visits. When we're together I feel that we're all on the same wavelength. There is never an awkwardness that someone is not "with it" when we're together.

We experience the same kind of closeness with Bill and Audrey, whom I mentioned earlier. We may not see each other for years. Yet the moment we're together, it seems as though we've never been apart. Yes, we need to catch up on news. But when we're together, I feel that we're all on the same wavelength. The reason is that Bill and Audrey are great friends with each other, just as Fay and I are great friends. We all feel close to each other because of the strength of the friendship in our own marriages.

There may be some truth to the "Great American Couple Friendship Fiction." But the reason is not found in the impossibility of two couples being four friends. It is because many married couples are not friends with each other. Two couples can be four friends only when the two couples are first and foremost friends with each other.

CHAPTER SEVEN
Singles' Friendships

Friendship is very important to singles. Having grown away from family of origin and not being married, they develop new relationships, commonly called "friendships." But therein lies a complication.

FRIEND OR FAMILY? Many "friendships" between singles, particularly those of the same sex, are not friendships at all. They are what Lewis describes as "need-love" relationships and as such deserve to be called intimacy, not friendship. In fact, singles often call these new people in their lives "family," which connotes a very special kind of relationship. One single woman put it to me this way:

> I still love and appreciate my biological family, but my emotional needs for sharing, for intimacy, for knowing and being known, are met by my friends. In one sense I do not need any one of them exclusively; in another sense, I need them all.

> Singles, more so than married people, need a wide circle of friends and acquaintances for support. Singles are no less "needy" than are married people—they just meet their needs in alternative ways. The more they are supported by many people who love them, the less likely they are to fall prey to their own neediness, or to someone else's unhealthy need for them. They also will have a stronger emotional base from which to build relationships in which eventually their needs may be met primarily by one trustworthy person (a spouse).

This is good! Indeed, it is healthy. But we ought not to call these need-love relationships *friendships*. I have three reasons for saying that.

First, as we have already seen, *need* is incidental to friendship. Friends will meet the needs of friends, but that's not what friendship is about. With intimacy, however, there is a *burden of intimacy*. If I permit you to *need* me, then I must be ready to be there for you when you come to me with your need.

From what the woman above told me about her "friendships" it sounds like they have worked out some agreement (possibly tacit) whereby they meet each other's needs. But one of the dangers of confusing intimacy and friendship is that needs may be created without there being an agreement to meet those needs.

Second, confusing friendship and intimacy can play havoc with the biological family (family of origin). This was Kenny's problem.

Kenny's sister, Molly, who never married, left home when she was twenty-one, and established relationships in her new hometown. She made no secret of the fact that these new people in her life were her "family" and she treated them with more deference than she did her family of origin.

Molly has drawn up a will naming her new "family" the beneficiaries of her very modest estate. Kenny has no problem with this. His question to me was, "What happens when Molly no longer is able to take care of herself? What happens when she is seventy years old, doesn't have much money, and will be indigent if she becomes ill. Is her new 'family' going to take care of her needs? I don't want a repeat of what happened with my father."

He then told me the story of his father, who divorced his mother and remarried. When he remarried he rarely contacted Kenny and Molly and, instead, made his second wife's family (children and grandchildren) his new family. When his father's wife died, one of her children called and told Kenny to come and get his father and take care of him.

"I can't tell you how much I resented that," Kenny told me. "If they had become his family—and such a *wonderful* family—why didn't *they* take care of him? They were real close until he became old and helpless and needed someone to take care of him. Then he winds up on my doorstep! There's something wrong when people are so very tight with each other until there's a need for constant care."

Kenny was afraid that this was going to happen with his sister. "I can just imagine them saying to me, 'We're her friends, not her family; you are. It's time to come and get her and take care of her.' If people are going to call each other family, then let them take on family responsibility!"

Third, confusing friendship and intimacy opens the door to problems when singles consider marriage. They develop an intimate relationship with the opposite sex, which they call a friendship. But it really is intimacy without the burden of intimacy. They never get to the altar because the relationship ends in hurt and distrust.

Kendra and Bill are one example. Kendra would never date Bill, but not because he's unattractive. In fact, he's the super stud of the singles group in her church. Whenever she has romantic thoughts about a man she thinks of Bill. But she doesn't trust him. He's too slick. He never can be pinned down as having specific convictions nor does anyone know what he's up to. He has a knack for finding out what people want and for holding out the promise of meeting their needs. But he usually winds up disappointing those expectations, getting more than he gives, and leaving others feeling used.

The singles' potluck was a small but good example. Everyone was supposed to bring something. Bill brought Kentucky Fried Chicken—not a whole bucket, but six pieces. When the group sat down to eat he consumed his six pieces of chicken and a whole lot more. But he couldn't see that he had effectively contributed nothing to the meal, even when others called it to his attention. Kendra then told me the following story.

"One night at a singles' meeting several weeks later Bill

took me aside and asked if he could talk to me after the meeting. Since one of our group's objectives was to encourage Christian friendship, I felt I owed it to him.

"I feel like there's a barrier between us," Bill began. "I'd like to get to know you as a friend, but whenever I'm around you, you seem cool and distant."

Kendra said, "I felt uneasy about his approaching me, partly because I found him attractive and partly because I distrusted him. But I felt that I couldn't turn down his bid for friendship. I pretended nothing was wrong. I told him that I'm just shy around guys, and of course I'd be his friend.

"This began a series of events," continued Kendra, "that for want of a better term began to erode my suspicion of him. Though we never dated, he always sat next to me in group functions and in church, was attentive to me, hilarious to be with, and always a gentleman. Though our stated relationship was friendship, I found a change taking place in my feelings. I began to look forward to being with him and having him sit next to me. I couldn't help responding to his attention, humor, and courtesy. I began to think that maybe he really could be a friend and that he really wasn't the 'Slick Willy' that I had once thought.

"One of my girlfriends picked up on my change of feeling toward Bill. She asked, 'What's with you and Bill? Do you have something going with each other that I don't know about?' I told her, 'Don't be silly. We're just friends.' And I honestly believed it. We never went out on a date or never so much as held hands." After several moments of thoughtfulness Kendra said, "I guess it's what you call a shoulder-to-shoulder relationship becoming a face-to-face relationship. Neither of us said anything, but we both knew it. Officially, we were just friends.

"I live near the church, and Bill began to walk home with me after activities. One night we were standing outside my condo talking about how close we had gotten to each other over the previous few months. We talked about our great 'friendship.' But I knew it was more than friendship. We were emotionally inseparable. You talk about 'need-love.' We needed each other, or so I thought. I know I needed Bill.

"Standing outside in front of my condo we kissed. It started gently, and before I knew what was happening it was a raging passion. My feelings surprised me. I hadn't planned on anything like that, and was a little embarrassed. I said I had to go, and beat a retreat to my apartment.

"That was the beginning of sorrows. We never talked about that kiss or the many kisses after that, and we continued to tell each other and the singles group that we were just good friends. After all, we never went out on a date. Sometimes I wondered if it was because Bill was too cheap, but I cared too much about him to think that of him.

"We spent a lot of time at my apartment eating, watching TV—and necking. Sometimes it got pretty hot. We never had sexual intercourse, but one night after an especially sizzling time on the sofa I asked Bill, 'Where is our relationship going?'

"He sat up, looked at me quizzically and said, 'What do you mean?'

"I said, 'Bill, I'm falling in love with you, and I want to know what the future holds for us.'

"I'll never forget Bill's reply or how he delivered it. He grasped my shoulders and said quietly, 'Kendra, all I ever wanted was to be your friend.'

"When he said that it instantly became clear that there was no future in this relationship, and I saw red. I held open my unbuttoned blouse and said, 'Is this what you do with a friend? It was just recreational kissing and fondling, wasn't it? It had no more meaning to you than that!'

"Bill stood up, and as he put on his jacket to leave he said gravely, as though I had wounded him deeply, 'I never said I wanted anything more than friendship with you. I'm sorry it has to end like this.' With that, he left."

That was the end of Kendra and Bill, but Kendra is still a very angry and distrustful woman many years later.

Several years after Kendra told me this story, I related it in a singles' seminar in another city (changing the names and places, of course). I was surprised at the response of a young woman in the front row. She said, "The woman was completely wrong. Her friend never told her he loved her and always maintained that it was a friendship. She read into the relationship something that wasn't there."

I stepped out from behind the lectern, went up to her, knelt down, took her hand, and kissed it. She blushed and giggled uneasily as the rest of the group howled with laughter. Holding her hand and looking closely into her eyes I said, "Hi. What's your name?" She said, "Julie," looked down, and laughed. Still holding my face close to hers (by now she had broken off eye contact and was attempting to suppress her giggles), I said, "Julie, I want to be your friend. Will you be my friend?" She didn't answer. She just looked down and giggled. I kissed her hand again and returned to the lectern.

The group screamed with delight and clapped. After they had quieted down I asked, "How credible was my bid for friendship?" The consensus was that I had definitely sent a double message. It was difficult *not* to read into what I had done an intention that went beyond friendship. The opinion of the group was summed up by a young woman who shouted from the back of the group, "The relationship's hot but the commitment's not!"

Unfortunately Kendra's experience is not unusual. I could tell many more stories of friendship proffered, but only as a cover for the exploitation of a need—sometimes sexual, sometimes financial, sometimes merely emotional.

Bob and Janet are another example of problems that arise when singles fail to distinguish between friendship and intimacy. Women are not the only ones who are hurt when this happens.

A frequent complaint I get from single men is that women will call them friends but will accept, and even ask for, a great deal of help from the men. It suggests to the men that they may have more than friendship going for them.

Janet, a professional woman, was always very busy around the house whenever she invited Bob over. She got him to help her do things she couldn't do—clean gutters, move furniture, and change the oil in her car. He even did some remodeling on her house, charging her nothing for his labor and only the cost of the material. She always gave him a nice meal when he was there and was nice company when they watched TV together in the evening.

Though there was no physical intimacy, Bob fell in love with Janet. But she didn't love Bob. She did enjoy the comfortable feeling she had when he was around. And all the things he did for her made her demanding life a lot easier.

Bob told me, "I knew she didn't love me, but I thought that if I made myself indispensable to her, she'd learn to love me. And the fact that she was willing to let me do for her all that I was doing said to me that she was open to having our relationship blossom into marriage.

"Things went on for a couple of years like this. I kept hoping that she would learn to love me, but it never happened. I began to get frustrated, and then angry. I started counting what our relationship had cost me. I had given an awful lot to this woman, and though she thanked me for what I had given, that was all I got.

"Call me old fashioned, but when a man buys a woman an expensive gift or he spends a great deal of time and effort meeting her needs—and she accepts—she is implying that there is a future in their relationship.

"I finally told Janet how I felt, and she got very defensive. She told me that she had never demanded anything of me or promised anything. But she sure took whatever I had to offer her. She just can't see that when a woman permits a man to do for her what I have done that he's going to feel that she has led him on and that she has been dishonest about the relationship."

WHEN TO TALK ABOUT YOUR FRIENDSHIP. Though friends don't usually talk about their friendship, because true friendship is about something besides themselves, friends better talk, and talk honestly when there is a hint that things are moving from friendship to intimacy, from appreciative-love to need-love. This is particularly true with singles who often begin relationships like Kendra and Bill's.

Kendra tried to talk by asking where the relationship was going. By so doing she was addressing an issue they hadn't talked about. Their emotionally intimate (and sexually tinged) behavior proved that they were more than just friends. They didn't just appreciate each other. They were developing an emotional *need* for each other.

When this happens, and there is a willingness on the part of both to talk about where the relationship is going, it can be a healthy state of affairs. But they must mutually agree that the relationship includes not only appreciative-love (friendship) but also need-love (intimacy). If you are going to let me *need* you and you *accept* my need of you, then I want some kind of a commitment that you will be there for me in my need.

In a developing romance, the stages of commitment are limited and gradual. Initially, they may agree to date each other exclusively, and when they find they are compatible they announce a formal engagement where they go on public record that they are considering marriage (and they receive pre-marital counseling), and then they make the final commitment to marry.

At any point in the process they should be assessing the viability of their relationship and agreeing whether it's working or not working. They are talking about their relationship because they are more than friends. They have declared to each other feelings of need that go beyond friendship. At any point either of them has the right to terminate further pursuit of marriage. Though it will be painful if one wants to continue and the other does not, it is less painful than a deceitful friendship or an inadvisable marriage.

Often I have been asked, "Can't they go back to being just

friends? No, I don't think so. Sometimes that happens, but if you have experienced deep emotional intimacy, it will be difficult to maintain a shoulder-to-shoulder relationship. You will continue to look at each other and wonder from time to time it if might have worked. Those feelings often precipitate a renewed effort to make the romance work, but when you continue to run into the same roadblocks you ran into before, you finally break off all contact, even friendship, because it's so exhausting to deal with your romantic feelings for each other.

Though friends sometimes do decide to marry, I find that when those marriages don't work it's because they never "caught fire." A sexual chemistry never developed and you find that you're married to someone who offers no more excitement than a brother or sister.

Of course the opposite also is true. Frequently, people "in love" marry, and when the passion and newness of marriage loses its excitement they discover that they have nothing else to share. They never developed a friendship.

Whenever I do premarital counseling I include the Couples Friendship Inventory described in chapter 8. When I find friendship lacking, I encourage them to delay marriage and work on becoming better friends.

Sometimes engaged couples think they are good friends because they are able to turn a blind eye to each other's faults and respect each other. But all too often I find that they do this not because they're such great friends but because *romantic love is blind!* Their acceptance of each other is based on fantasy rather than real knowledge of what the other person is like.

Friends are well-aware of one another's faults but are able to turn a blind eye because they are convinced of each other's commitment to their common vision. Couples *must* be able to do this if their marriages are to survive. Far better to realistically face each other's faults before marriage than face the prospect of losing a marriage because you never learned how to be friends.

UNREALISTIC EXPECTATIONS OF FRIENDSHIP. Singles sometimes have problems with their friendships because they have unrealistic expectations. There is no intention on anybody's part to mislead. It rises out of a misunderstanding of the nature of friendship. They don't understand that friendship is not the place to find intimacy—the fulfillment of need-love.

Need-love, historically, was found in the family—either the family of origin or in the establishment of a new family as two singles marry. But what happens when a single person has a need for intimacy, but is not near his family of origin or is unable or unwilling to marry?

Sharon is a fitting example. She is thirty-one, divorced, and has no children. She would like to remarry but is afraid of making another bad choice. So she remains single—and very lonely. "I need friends," she said. "But I just can't find meaningful and lasting relationships."

Sharon's statement of need and the history of her relationships reveal that she needs more than friends. She needs affirmation, affection, warmth, and loyalty—all the "warm fuzzies" found in a relationship more intimate than friendship. She is starved for love. "I just need someone to hug me," she said. "I want to know that people care about me—that I'm really important to them, that they need me as much as I need them."

Sharon's relationships have never lasted. Every time someone showed friendship, she took the relationship beyond mere appreciative-love. She spent so much time, energy, and money pursuing the friend with the hope that this person would reciprocate with equal personal interest that she alienated every one of them.

"Why can't I keep friends?" she moaned. I pointed out that she lost them because she made it evident that *she wanted more than friends.* They were willing to reciprocate at the appreciative-love level, but they were not willing to make commitments required by need-love.

If friendship is appreciative-love rather than need-love, it is a contradiction of terms to say we "need" friends. We may *enjoy* friends, but we *need* affection, warmth, and affirmation for emotional survival. What does a single person do to get need-love, particularly a Christian single who is unwilling to get into uncommitted intimacies with the opposite sex?

Intimacy is usually established in family relationships where there is commitment and where we enjoy the rewards of intimacy in exchange for the burden of intimacy. Such intimacy comes from our family of origin—parents, grand-parents, brothers, sisters, aunts, uncles, and cousins—or from a family of our own that we establish in marriage. Sharon, like many other singles, is away from her family of origin and has no opportunity to establish a family of her own, because the prospects of marriage are dim.

It's not only singles like Sharon who are caught in this dilemma, however. Some singles don't wish to marry, yet feel a need for nonsexual intimacy. How does a single fulfill intimacy needs when he or she is away from family of origin or when there is no hope of or desire for marriage?

DISTINGUISHING FRIENDSHIP FROM INTIMACY. Sharon needed to distinguish between friendship and intimacy. She had to see that friends are not necessary but intimates are. She had to understand that nonsexual intimacy, such as affirmation, affection, warmth, loyalty, and involvement can only be fulfilled by someone's *commitment*. Here we return to the burden of intimacy—even nonsexual intimacy. Meaningful and lasting relationships are based on commit-ments. Those commitments must be openly discussed by all the people involved.

Sharon had a way of ingratiating herself to couples or older singles, getting "adopted" as a surrogate daughter, and then becoming very demanding of their time and energy. She was not assertive, but instead came across as a poor, loveless soul. She made people feel sorry for her until they began to feel used. Then the relationships cooled off.

People really couldn't be friends with Sharon, because she

needed more than friends. But her emotional needs went so deep that it was difficult to establish a family intimacy with her—her expectations were greater than any individual or couple were willing to commit themselves to.

Sharon's intimacy needs could be met if she first thoroughly discussed her expectations with the people she sought intimacy with. Then she needed to find out what they were willing to do in the way of commitment to her. Sharon's commitment also needed to be defined. For example, she may be invited to drop in at particular times with the understanding that 10:00 P.M. was the time to go home. Limits could be placed on the frequency and length of phone calls between them. She had free access to the refrigerator and pantry, but she was expected to clean up the kitchen and put her dishes in the dishwasher.

In exchange for these commitments, what was she willing to commit to the family? What part of herself was she willing to give up for them? Too often, singles looking for warmth and intimacy with another person, a couple, or a family tend to think in terms of what *they* need and what they are going to get from the relationship rather than what they are going to bring into it. For true intimacy there must be reciprocity. Many of Sharon's relationships ended because she cultivated an individual or couple who had much to offer her, but they never talked about what she was going to give to them. Sharon's biggest mistake was choosing intimates for what she could get from them rather than what she could give them.

In addition, Sharon often chose people who, while having much to offer her, could get along quite well without her. There was no need of reciprocity, and therefore the relationship died. True intimacy requires that the intimates *need* each other and are willing to meet those needs.

Commitment, the quality that distinguishes intimacy from friendship, is the issue. What is the single willing to commit of *herself* in return for the "warm fuzzies" that come from a reciprocal commitment? Here are some things a single can do:

- *"Adopt" a person who has bad eyesight or is blind, and read to him and be his eyes.*
- *"Adopt" a shut-in and attend to his needs and be company to him.*
- *Provide transportation for a person who has none, especially to the market or to the doctor.*
- *Offer ongoing emotional solace to someone who is bereaved.*
- *Visit someone in the hospital and follow up on him when he has been released to be sure that recovery has been complete.*
- *Open your home (meals included) to someone who is alone.*
- *Mow the grass or shovel the snow for an older person who has no one to do it for him. Be attentive to that person's similar ongoing needs.*
- *Take a casserole to a home where there is illness and be attentive to their needs until there is complete recovery.*
- *Provide transportation to church for someone who is without. Use this time to cultivate him in matters of faith.*
- *"Adopt" a Bible college student and send him money and encouragement regularly. Invite him to your home.*
- *Help clean house for someone who isn't well. If the condition is chronic, develop a long-term relationship.*
- *Offer to care for the children of a young mother so she can be relieved of the constant demand of parenting. This is especially important for solo parents.*
- *Find a child whose absent parent's role you can help to fill. Invite him to activities that would interest him.[1]*

In response to this someone said to me, "You imply that one can have more intimacy with a shut-in than with a close friend. Intimacy is knowing and being known. Although committing ourselves to helping others who are less fortunate may increase our capacity to love, it doesn't necessarily result in intimacy."

I reply that knowing and being known rises out of a need-love relationship. The giver and getter reward each other emotionally by fulfilling each other's needs and in the process get to know each other and each other's needs better. But I cannot have intimacy with a person who doesn't need me. I may need him, but if he doesn't need me, the relationship will soon cool off because it is so one-sided.

This is why commitment is necessary in intimacy or need-love relationships. If our relationship develops to the point that I *need* you, then to keep from being hurt I should know whether or not I have a commitment from you to be there in my time of need.

Another single woman said to me, "Sharon's problem was that she concentrated all of her needs on a few people. She needed a wider circle of friends." No, she didn't need a wider circle of friends. She needed a wide circle of *intimates*.

The fact is that Sharon had a wide circle of friends. But she had ruined those friendships because she didn't understand that getting needs met is *incidental* to friendship. Lewis puts it well when he says that friendship will help when the pinch comes,

> But that, having been given, it makes no difference at all. It was a distraction, an anomaly. It was a horrible waste of the time, always too short, that we had together. Perhaps we had only a couple of hours in which to talk and, God bless us, twenty minutes of it has had to be devoted to affairs.[2]

What Sharon needed was a wider circle of intimates who were willing to become a family to her. It was Sharon's inability to make a distinction between friendship and intimacy that got her in trouble.

The distinction between the two is not mere semantics. The distinction is vital to the way people relate to each other. The meeting of needs is incidental to friendship but it is the heart and soul of intimacy. To impose need on friendship can kill it—as it did in Sharon's case.

ESTABLISHING YOUR OWN IDENTITY. For the single person to engage in reciprocal intimacy, he must have an identity of his own to share. The idea that we are incomplete until we are married is unbiblical. In fact, a single person is in a better position than a married person to serve God and his church (1 Cor. 7:32–35). The church is in big trouble if singles are "incomplete" people, because they have a vital role in its ministry.

The best way to get intimacy is to give it. The only way we can give it is to have identities of our own. A large part of that identity comes by establishing our own home and surroundings—that personal touch in our homes that is uniquely *us*. One writer put it well when she said that the single life need not and should not be a makeshift affair. She said that a single woman is in a position to give of herself and to use her home and her resources to offer to others what she is looking for herself—affection, affirmation, loyalty, and warmth.[3]

Establishing a home on this basis need not be viewed as an attempt to snare a husband—though an eligible man might be impressed by what such a woman has to offer. She could open her home to older men and women whose children have deserted them and who are hungry to get and give love. A single woman might fulfill her maternal instinct by bringing children into her home. She could become a foster parent; social service agencies need foster parents desperately. This means *commitment*. Without commitment there is no intimacy.

The single who wants a meaningful and lasting relationship that involves emotional needs must ask, "What do I have to offer to this person in terms of my own commitment? How much of my time, energy, talent, and money am I willing to commit to this person in order to experience the intimacy I desire? Emotional intimacy, like sexual intimacy, will not last without commitment.

CAROLYN LOVES TONY. A remarkable example of such commitment by a single person is found in Carolyn's love for Tony. Carolyn Koons, now more than fifty years old, was, at the time the story began, a professor of Christian education at Azusa Pacific College in California. One of the things that Carolyn did was to take groups of high-school and college students to Mexico to minister.

In 1975, on one of her trips to the border town of Mexicali, the chaplain of the men's prison asked Carolyn to visit the boys' prison nearby. There her group saw three hundred boys, ranging in age from five to eighteen, incarcerated like common criminals.

While ministering to the boys, she discovered ten-year-old Antonio (Tony). He was in prison for murder though he never had been tried. One night five years earlier, the police had been called to investigate the death of Tony's eighteen-month-old sister. His mother told the police that Tony had beaten his sister to death.

The police took Tony into custody at 2:00 A.M. and told his mother to come in at 8:00, when the records office opened, to give a statement. When she didn't show up, the police realized that Tony had not killed his sister—his mother had. They also discovered that Tony had been a victim of abuse—his body was covered with scars—and that his mother, a prostitute, had abandoned or killed his six other brothers and sisters before this tragedy.

Though innocent, Tony was placed in the boys' prison and had been there for about five years when Carolyn discovered him. She felt that God had led her to him, and she knew just the couple to adopt him—a young Spanish-speaking woman and her husband who worked with juveniles. They agreed to adopt Tony if Carolyn could arrange it.

Through incredible tenacity, Carolyn saw to it that Tony

was proved innocent of the crime, and she began to attack the mountain of paperwork to get him out of Mexico. For two and a half years she faced delay after delay—including obstructionism by the prison's director. When she finally completed the paperwork, the prospective parents decided they didn't want to adopt Tony—they now had two children of their own.

Carolyn went to other couples, but no one wanted a twelve-year-old Mexican boy who had been in prison. At age thirty-five, Carolyn was faced with the meaning of commitment. Yes, she had done missionary work in Mexico and had given herself to a life of service for Christ. But she had always been able to go home to comfortable California and the freedom of her singleness. Now a twelve-year-old boy was depending on her for survival—a boy nobody wanted. What could she do? They didn't speak the same language. He was from a vastly different culture. He had almost no education and couldn't even write his own name. But she said yes, she would adopt him.

That was only the beginning of Carolyn's troubles. It was even more difficult to get Tony out of Mexico than out of prison. He couldn't get a passport because he didn't have a birth certificate. But through God's intervention, a passport was issued.

Carolyn knew that the first year would be tough. She was willing to give up her freedom as a single. But she wasn't prepared for the violence that erupted from this troubled boy—violence that had been the means of survival in prison. It was all he knew. She was equally unprepared for his being expelled from school for violent behavior.

As the years passed and Carolyn lived out her commitment to Tony, he began to change. And she did too. The moment of triumph came when he graduated from the eighth grade. Carolyn was to speak at the graduation ceremonies, and Tony asked if he could say something to the audience. With Carolyn sitting on the platform behind him, Tony said, "I want to thank my mom for adopting me and taking me out of Mexico. It's the greatest thing that ever happened to me." Then he turned, threw his arms around Carolyn, and said, "I love you! I love you!"

Reflecting on that moment, Carolyn said, "It all came together: the memories of prison, the battle to get him out, the struggle we had had making it as mother and son, the times I thought we wouldn't make it. When he threw his arms around me and said, 'I love you,' it was all worth it."

Carolyn had that moment to treasure—a boy's undying love for her. Why? Because she was willing to invest her life in Tony—to *commit* her time, money, talents, and prayers to this boy. For the single person wanting meaningful and lasting relationships, Carolyn's story asks the question, "What are *you* willing to commit to make it possible?"[4]

CHAPTER EIGHT

Making Your Mate Your Best Friend

The emancipation of women has increased the opportunity for opposite-sex friendships. But there's another reason for the growing number of male-female relationships. Couples are having difficulty finding friendship in marriage—so they seek it elsewhere.

Take the case of Jerry, age thirty-eight. Jerry doesn't have any close male friends because friendship means vulnerability. He believes that men tend to take advantage of vulnerability, which they see as weakness. So his closest friend is a woman. "She knows me better than my wife does, more than any man does," Jerry says. "It's easier to express weakness to a woman than to a man, because it's acceptable. She's open and receptive to my feelings, and I'm never afraid of her using my vulnerability to hurt me. I never worry about retaliation."

Jerry says that he has a good marriage and that he loves his family. But home is not where he is nurtured by a friend. Jerry feels he's carrying a burden—even at home. "It's me against the world. . . . I can't even ease up at home; I always have to be 'on.' With my woman friend I can be off-guard. . . ."[1]

JERRY'S WIFE ISN'T HIS FRIEND

Jerry reveals a great deal about his marriage by what he says. There's no doubt he loves his wife and she him, but they are not friends.

He reveals this in several statements: feeling a burden, always having to be "on" at home, and feeling unable to be off-guard at home. It is not clear how much of this Jerry is responsible for or how much is due to his family's demands. But it raises some important questions. Does Jerry feel that his wife's respect for him is based on his accomplishments? What will happen if he slows down? Does Jerry feel that his wife's need for financial security is so great that he can't let up on his work? Is Jerry's wife so emotionally insecure and dependent on him that he must be a tower of strength all the time?

My experience with couples is that, more often than not, the man puts these burdens on himself. A wife may unwittingly reinforce the burden with expressions of dismay or concern about her husband's dissatisfaction with his job or the pressure that's on him. But most wives do not base love and respect for their husbands on accomplishment. They may be proud of their husbands' achievements. But achievement or success is not the basis of respect.

If a husband says that he is tired of the rat race and would like to take a new direction, a wife may show concern. But it's not usually *her* security needs that keep him in the rat race. It's *his* security needs. It's his male ego that measures his self-worth by his accomplishments.

Often the wife believes that her husband wants a demanding job with the financial reward that goes with it. So she gears her life and the family's to his job and its demands and schedule. But then she's blamed for being a burden to him— as though *she* has all these expectations of him.

If Jerry's wife is not his friend, it may be because he won't let her be. It's easy for him to be weak and vulnerable with his woman friend, since she doesn't depend on him for her emotional and financial security. Why should she be alarmed or concerned if he's tired of the rat race and would rather be a sailing instructor than a highly paid salesman?

Jerry is unwilling to let his wife sort out her need-love and her appreciative-love by talking with her about his burden. Sure, she'll need to count the cost. But he must give her a chance to show that she can be a true friend by giving up her needs for his well-being.

YOUR SPOUSE AS FRIEND

How do we determine whether or not our spouses are our friends? Psychologist Everett Shostrom developed a helpful test called the "Caring Relationship Inventory." He maintains that true and lasting love is made up of a number of qualities measured by affection, eros, empathy, self-love, the ability to love a person for what he is rather than for what he does, and friendship. Love is viewed as a jewel with all these facets, and friendship is an important facet.

THE NATURE OF FRIENDSHIP IN MARRIAGE. Shostrom says that friendship in marriage is a peer love based on common interest and respect for each other's equality. Friends have common or complementary interests. They each appreciate the other's talents and worth. Divorcees, considering remarriage, value friendship in a relationship more than romance. It seems they want a buddy, not a sweetheart.[2]

Friendship in marriage can become manipulative, however. When we exploit or use our spouses for our own purposes, it is not friendship. It reveals a self-centeredness that is alien to friendship. A lack of appreciation for what our spouses freely do for us also shows a lack of friendship. When we feel that they *ought* to do for us what they are doing, where is the friendship—the *free* gift, the gift that goes beyond mere duty?

Remember that the word "free" is the root meaning of the

English word "friend." That which a friend does is done *freely* and not out of duty.

A common error I find in marriages, particularly in the husband's behavior, is that he expects so much of his wife that there is nothing left that can be given freely. The attitude often is, "You're not doing your *duty*." There is no place for friendship in that kind of marriage, because everything the wife does is considered to be duty.

COUPLES' FRIENDSHIP INVENTORY. Using Shostrom's inventory as a guide, I have formulated the following statements to help couples evaluate friendship in marriage. Under each statement I give an explanation of what is meant. Though I use the masculine pronoun in the explanation, the feminine pronoun should be understood when the husband is evaluating his wife. Each statement should be responded to on a scale of 1 to 5. A 5 response indicates that the quality is definitely found in the relationship. A 1 response indicates it definitely is not found. A 3 response is neither yes nor no. A 2 or 4 gives the respondent an opportunity to indicate a lesser degree of yes or no.

The purpose of this inventory is to give couples an opportunity to discuss the quality of their friendship in marriage. Spouses should take the inventory and compare their responses. Do they differ in their responses? If so, why?

The total scores give some indication of the strength or weakness of the friendship:

Very good friendship	73–85
Good friendship	60–72
Needs work	47–59
Poor friendship	34–46
Very poor friendship	17–33

No   Yes

1. I respect him/her.   1 2 3 4 5

Even though he is an individual in his own right, I feel an affinity with him. He may be unlike me, but even so, I feel that I complement him. We share common ideas, ideals, and activities, and I respect his approach to the things we have in common.

2. I like him/her as he/she is.   1 2 3 4 5

He doesn't have to be like me in order for me to like him. I feel a common bond with him and admire the way he thinks and acts.

3. I could live without him/her, but
   my life would be poorer for it.   1 2 3 4 5

One of the things I value about him is the richness he brings to my life. I could get along without him if I had to, but knowing him brings pleasure to my life. His value to me is more than just emotional or physical survival.

4. I enjoy sharing what we have in
   common with others of like mind.   1 2 3 4 5

Though my relationship with him may be exclusive as far as emotional and sexual intimacy are concerned, the two of us enjoy like-minded people who share the ideas and ideals we hold in common.

5. If we were not married, we would
   still share a lot of the same ideas,
   ideals, and activities.   1 2 3 4 5

Our marriage involves a number of things such as emotional intimacy and sexual attraction. But we would still be friends even if not married because of the ideas, ideals, and activities we have in common.

6. I respect him/her even when he/she does things that upset or annoy me.   1 2 3 4 5

Our relationship is not based solely on my comfort or pleasure but on a common bond and a view of life that surpasses personal gratification.

7. I know him/her well enough that I can anticipate what his/her words or behavior will be in most circumstances.   1 2 3 4 5

Because we share common ideas and ideals I can tell how he will react in most circumstances. That reaction will be consistent with the way I know he looks at life.

8. It's easy to turn a blind eye to his/her faults.   1 2 3 4 5

Because we share a common vision, it's easy to overlook minor and occasional failures to live up to it.

9. I want what is best for him/her.   1 2 3 4 5

My relationship with him is not based solely on the gratification of my own needs, but also on a sincere desire to have him experience what is best for him.

10. I care enough to let him/her go or even give him/her up.   1 2 3 4 5

I am willing to sacrifice my own needs if letting him go is in his best interest.

11. My respect for him/her is *not*
    based on his/her accomplishments.   1 2 3 4 5

The basis of my respect is his fidelity to the ideas and ideals that we hold in common. He could achieve less and still be my friend.

12. I know he/she is a kindred spirit
    even though I may not be assured
    frequently that he/she is.   1 2 3 4 5

Because our kindred spirit is felt and demonstrated in many little ways, I don't need frequent assurance that it's there.

13. He/she seems to bring out the best
    in me.   1 2 3 4 5

Because we share common ideas and ideals, when I am with him I find that my thinking about and expression of these things are stimulated by him.

14. I feel that we stand together
    against the views of outsiders.   1 2 3 4 5

Views of others that run contrary to the way we think tend to unite, rather than divide us.

15. I can be both strong and weak
    with him/her.   1 2 3 4 5

Because we have mutual respect for each other, strength is not threatening nor is weakness despised.

16. My giving to him/her is character-
    ized by freedom and willingness
    and not grudging sacrifice.   1 2 3 4 5

Because I want what is best for him, I am willing to give freely without thought of its cost to me.

17. My relationship with him/her is
    characterized by trust.   1 2 3 4 5

I believe that his actions have my best interests at heart, that they are selfless in motive, and therefore I am able to trust him.

WHEN LOVERS BECOME FRIENDS

To achieve these ideals in marriage it's mandatory that we understand an important process of maturity in marriage— the process whereby lovers become friends. This was lacking in Sid's marriage.

When Sid married at age twenty-five he was desperately in love. Renee gave him an incredible high. Marriage was so great that he didn't want them to have any children for a while; he just wanted to enjoy her. But unexpectedly they did have a child. Then they decided to have another so the first one wouldn't be an only child.

As the years passed Sid felt that he and Renee were losing the romance in their marriage. He worked very hard to keep it by taking Renee to nightclubs and having candlelight dinners at home. But it seemed that no matter how hard they worked at romance, they were losing it.

Now he sat in my office despondent and confused. He had fallen out of love with Renee and in love with a woman at the office. He wondered what had happened to his high with Renee. "I guess it wasn't the real thing," he speculated. "This other woman gives me a high that I haven't felt in a long time. But how do I know if this is the real thing? I don't want to make the same mistake again." Sid's problem was that he had "the wretched habit of romance."

THE WRETCHED HABIT OF ROMANCE. It's usually women who are the incurable romantics. Snow White, Cinderella, Sleeping Beauty, and Rapunzel are among the more famous ones. They all believed that someday their prince would come; he did, and they lived happily ever after.

"Gothic" romance novels feed this fantasy. The beautiful girls on the book covers are shown being carried away by fantastically handsome men. They are swept out of their dungeons of despair by their princes and carried to dizzying heights of romance.

The problem with the Snow White stories and the Gothic novels is that they tend to promote the wretched habit of romance. This is the habit that looks for a nonstop tingle and excitement in life. It is the constant need for something wonderful to happen along with the fear, apprehension, and tension that go along with it to make it exciting.[3]

A romantic high is sexual, mental, and emotional. We need certain conditions in order to experience this high. Insecurity—I'm not sure if he cares as much about me as I care about him. Curiosity—he's a bit mystifying, unpredictable. Barriers—other people such as a spouse, children, or co-workers. Limits—how much time we have together. They're all there: Mystery, insecurity, barriers, limits—and *magic*. The magic is that unspoken electric experience when two people look at each other and know what the other is thinking.

There are many kinds of highs—work, the accomplishments of our children, or our avocation. There's nothing wrong with wanting an exciting life. But when our highs come only from *romantic* involvement, we're headed for disappointment. People who think they're happy only when they're "in love" are enslaved by the wretched habit of romance.[4]

THE HAPPINESS MYTH. Americans are preoccupied with being happy. My office is filled with people who have come to the place in their lives where they're not happy. What complicates things is that they feel—justifiably so—that they have nothing to be unhappy about.

What's the problem? It's the happiness myth. We think something's wrong if we're not happy every day. But happy is not ordinary. It's extraordinary. Happy means ecstatic. It is not a normal state of affairs. It's occasional. The opposite of happy is blah, which, again, is not ordinary but occasional. Most of us live middle-of-the-road lives that are *comfortable*.

Comfortable is sipping a cup of coffee with my wife as we slowly wake up in the morning and watch summer come to life around us. Comfortable is looking across the room at each other as we try to wake up and laughing together at being such zombies. Comfortable is waking up quietly—no need to say anything but just smiling and sighing. Comfortable is sitting in front of a fire in wintertime, hearing the wind and watching the falling snow with someone who is easy to be with. Comfortable is sharing dreams and fantasies without fear of criticism or fear that my mate may take away from the relationship by indulging some private, unspoken need.

There's comfortable sex too. Most of the time it's not the high we knew on our honeymoon. Sometimes it is. But neither of us is a mystery to the other anymore. The excitement of mystery and discovery have now been replaced with something equally rewarding—comfort.

The myth of happiness is destructive because it robs us of the greatest reward of friendship in marriage—comfort. We wake up one morning and don't feel any excitement. We drink our coffee together, but there's no tingle of expectation or tension of anticipation. In forty-two years of marriage we have sipped breakfast coffee together 15,330 times. Instead of appreciating and valuing the comfort, we decide that the absence of tingle, expectation, and delightful tension means we're not happy.

It may be helpful to know that we're not supposed to be happy. We're supposed to be comfortable. Happy is a high; it's something out of the ordinary. The norm is *comfort*. It's when we think the norm ought to be a daily high that we decide life is blah.

If we're honest with ourselves we have to admit that life is not blah. Yes, some days are blah. But they are infrequent. Some days are high. But most days are comfortable.

The happiness myth is why men and women, after many years of marriage, throw away perfectly good comfort relationships. They think they want each day to be a high. But when they throw away that comfortable marriage in pursuit of a high with someone else, they discover that the new relationship also loses its mystery and excitement. They become the sad souls we see moving from one relationship to the next, seeking that eternal high. They are constantly in pursuit of that elusive "real love" that they believe will give them ecstasy every day of their lives.

This was Sid's problem. He left his wife, but after a few hundred days of sipping morning coffee with another person, he discovered that the tingle was gone again. Sid, in pursuit of his high—"real love"—is now on his third marriage. He is an example of a person who does not understand that real love is made up of a number of qualities, among them the comfort that's found in a lover who has become a friend.

PRACTICAL WAYS TO CULTIVATE FRIENDSHIP

Couples who are interested in developing their friendship can take these positive steps.

First, take the Couples' Friendship Inventory without consulting each other. After you're done, each of you should go through the inventory item by item saying how you scored it and why. This can make it a rewarding and informing exercise. You may be pleased to discover that your mate has positive feelings about you that you were not aware of. When the feelings are less than positive, be careful not to discount them. Don't say, "You shouldn't feel that way because. . . ."

If your mate gives you a less than flattering rating, try to understand why he or she feels that way without defending yourself. Find out what changes you can make that would make your mate feel differently.

Second, look for patterns in the response. A fundamental element of friendship is a common vision. Do you consistently give your mate a low score because you feel that a common vision is lacking in your marriage? Perhaps each of you has a different idea of where you want to be five, ten, or twenty years from now. Listen to each other's vision of the future, and look for common elements in each vision that the two of you can share.

What do you say on the inventory about respect? Are you able to respect each other because you each believe in the other's commitment to the vision? Are you able to overlook one another's faults because you are convinced of each other's commitment to your vision?

Because the shared vision of friends is so important, they must be accessible to talk to one another. Do you have a time when the two of you just sit and talk about your hopes and dreams?

Fay and I have the kind of schedule that allows us to start our mornings slowly. We get a cup of coffee, sit down and we talk about what we have to do that day. Often we talk about how our immediate plans fit into the larger plan for the week, or month. This is the time we talk about our frustrations and identify those things that are keeping us from our vision. It also gives us an opportunity to check and see if we're working together.

How accessible are you to each other throughout the day when you're at home together? We have made it a practice that whenever we're reading or watching TV and the other one comes into the room, we will put down what we're reading or turn down the TV to see if the other one has come to talk.

Friends talk to each other about their common vision and the things that must happen to make it work. They share good news when the vision shows promise of becoming reality. They share the concern over those things that keep the vision from happening.

It is this kind of sharing that makes friendship in marriage work. It makes marriage comfortable and gives a sense that you're together in making your life work. This feeling is all important to couples as they grow older and must depend on each other for the fulfillment of their common vision.

CHAPTER NINE
When There's Someone Else

Most marriages will, at some time, be threatened by some form of third-party intimacy. Sometimes it will result in sexual infidelity. Numerous polls have been taken to determine how many married people have had extramarital intercourse. Anywhere from 21 to 54 percent of wives cheat on their husbands, depending on which ladies' magazine is taking the poll.[1] For men, the figure is usually higher. That's due more to logistics than lust, because men get out of the house more than women do.[2]

No polls have been taken on how many marriages have been disrupted by emotional infidelity and alienation of affection. An educated guess is that nine out of ten marriages have experienced a disruption from a "close encounter of the third kind."

I dimly recall my mother giving my father grief about their good friend Mildred. Mildred and George were a couple they socialized with when I was a child. I was friends with their son, Myron. Our families were close. I can't remember what Mother said, but I do remember being startled by her emotional outburst. I asked my eighty-four-year-old father about this before he died, and he just chuckled and said, "Oh yes, Mildred! She'd chase anything with pants on," and dismissed it at that.

But not everyone can chuckle or be as philosophical as Dad. Many husbands and wives are deeply hurt by spouses who felt it was necessary to get close to someone else.

A POLYGAMOUS SOCIETY

Some who cheat on their spouses simply declare that we live in a polygamous society. For example, a poll taken by the Institute for Advanced Study of Human Sexuality showed that one-half of the women polled seemed to feel that sexual relations are not governed by marriage vows. Forty percent declared themselves "naturally polygamous."[3]

The fact is that polygamous societies have rules when it comes to multiple relationships. In Old Testament Israel, a concubine—usually a purchased slave or a captive from war—was considered a second wife and protected by law. For example, if a poverty-stricken father sold his daughter into slavery, she could be bought as a concubine. But she was not released after six years as male slaves were. This may have been because she had no means of support or its purpose might have been to maintain the integrity of the family for the sake of children born to the union. If the buyer of the slave decided he didn't want her, he could not sell her to foreigners. He had to permit another Jew to buy her and care for her (Exod. 21:1–11).

A man who gave a concubine as a gift to his son had to treat her as a daughter. If the son decided to take another woman as his wife, the concubine was still entitled to food, clothing, and all the marital rights. If she were not given these, she was given her freedom, which was a form of payment to her. Then she could go back to her own father's house and be cared for by him with the money he had gained from the original sale. The point is that concubines had rights under the law and were protected.

Protection was also accorded the captured foreign slave who became a concubine (Deut. 21:10–14). If she fell out of favor, she could not be sold as a slave but was given freedom. She was not turned out of the home with no means of support. That would have been more cruel than selling her as a slave to someone who would take care of her.[4]

Multiple wives were permitted in that culture. But those

who kept concubines became responsible for them and their children. A man could get rid of the concubine who bore his first child. But the child was not displaced and still had the rights of the firstborn (Deut. 21:15–17).

Polygamy in ancient Israel was an attempt to deal with secular prostitution. Though multiple sexual relations were permitted within the laws governing polygamy, extramarital relations were condemned and sometimes punished by death.[5]

The modern American who talks about polygamy really wants multiple sexual relations with no restraint and no rules. A polygamous society, however, has rules that govern multiple sexual relationships. Those who would impose rules are not just spoilsports.

WHY SPOUSES STRAY

The reason why spouses stray is more complex than a mere natural proclivity to polygamy. Straying may mean everything from emotional infidelity or alienation of affection to sexual relations.

SEXUAL INCOMPATIBILITY. Sometimes a spouse strays because of sexual incompatibility—real or imagined. One thirty-five-year-old woman sought a lover because her husband was impotent and was unwilling to do anything about his lack of sexual desire or ability.

A forty-two-year-old man, married a second time, resumed sexual relations with a former lover because, he said, "My new wife didn't show enough interest in me."[6]

REACTION TO REJECTION. Sometimes a husband or wife feels rejected by the other spouse. One woman in her late twenties had a brief affair after the birth of her third child because her husband didn't visit her in the hospital.

A man whose wife took an extended trip to her parents'

lavish summer home, leaving him to work in a hot city, had an affair with his secretary.[7]

COPING WITH MIDLIFE CRISIS. Approaching age forty for women or age fifty for men is a critical time of life. Waning attractiveness and a sense of mortality often spur the middle-aged to take one last fling at life. Even if they don't become sexually involved, they want their attractiveness affirmed by others besides their mates. One man said, "Of course my wife says I'm attractive. She's married to me." Her affirmation was discounted simply because he felt she was just doing her wifely duty.

HOSTILITY. Sometimes hostility, conscious or unconscious, leads a husband or wife to cultivate another relationship. A thirty-four-year-old mother of two children grew increasingly resentful over her husband's self-centeredness and lack of consideration. She got even by having an affair with her neighbor and letting her husband know about it.

Unconscious hostility usually shows up in a lack of affection and the inability to perform sexually. The motivation for getting involved with someone else, sexually or otherwise, may not be sexual fulfillment. It often is a demonstration of anger that is not expressed to the spouse.

The partners who are hurt by straying spouses and feel responsible for the damaged marriage should not chastise themselves too hastily. They can't do anything about hostility that is not verbalized. Sometimes they must wait for the third party to appear before the hostility is expressed and can be discussed.

LACK OF COMMUNICATION. Husbands and wives who get involved outside of marriage usually can't talk with their spouses about sensitive issues. So they find surrogates who will listen. The spouses left in the cold are hurt because things that ought to be discussed in the privacy of marriage are being discussed elsewhere. Such behavior is usually considered "emotional infidelity."

PERSISTENT COMPLEX SEXUAL PROBLEMS. A twenty-nine-year-old man was married, had good sexual relations with his wife, and they had children. But he continued a long history of picking up prostitutes. He excused himself on the grounds that he was "oversexed." In reality he had serious doubts about his masculinity and felt driven to prove himself through extramarital sexual activity. Only after he contracted venereal disease did he agree with his wife to get psychological help.[8]

LACK OF COMMITMENT. Some husbands and wives become involved with others sexually or emotionally because they are unwilling to commit themselves to their marriages. This is usually a sign of deep-rooted psychological problems.

Some spouses are so terrified by the closeness they feel in marriage that they must keep one foot outside the door in order to feel safe. Others are so independent that they use liaisons outside the marriage as a way of asserting that independence. Still others are so self-absorbed that they see no reason to be sexually or emotionally faithful. They go through their entire lives with the attitude, "I want what I want when I want it." Often these people have been raised by indulgent parents who led them to believe that the world revolves around them. Or they have been so emotionally deprived as children that they're determined to make up for it as adults.

Infidelity, whether sexual or emotional, doesn't always mean the wounded spouse has failed. But it does indicate a need to reexamine the marriage in terms of each other's needs.

Third-party friendship has its place in a well-ordered marriage because it is not an expression of *need*. Friendship is not *necessary*, though without it life might be a little poorer.

However, when interest in someone else is an expression of an unmet *need*, then it's time for the husband and wife to find out what is lacking in the marriage.

Jessie was troubled about Walter's relationship with a woman-friend in another state. This young woman had sought his counsel and guidance on a number of occasions, and Walter maintained that they had a father-daughter relationship. His reason for being with her was to give her spiritual guidance.

On one occasion Walter had to make a business trip to the city in which the young woman lived. Jessie was overwrought. As Walter prepared to go, it was evident that he was very anxious to get there. He even moved the trip up a day or two so he could arrive earlier. Jessie was convinced, justifiably, that Walter couldn't wait to see this woman. The relationship was not mere appreciative-love for a kindred spirit. Walter had betrayed a *need* to be with her.

We must not assume, however, that it's only opposite-sex relationships that disrupt marriages. Frequently men hurt their marriages by insisting on spending a great deal of time with their buddies. After-work hours and weekends are spent drinking and playing. And with the increasing number of women in the work force, women are beginning to do the same with their girlfriends. The message to the spouse left at home is that there's not much of interest to come home to. When such behavior is persistent, it reveals a serious lack in the marriage relationship.

JEALOUSY

The spouse who objects to friendships outside the marriage is often accused of jealousy. This emotion is considered to be unacceptable in a modern, enlightened marriage. The objecting spouse is told, "The problem is yours, not mine. If you weren't so jealous, we wouldn't have a problem."

Psychologists don't agree on the subject of jealousy. It has been described both as "a healthy and familiar expression of romantic love" and "a tragic characteristic of all people."[9] They do agree, however, that jealousy is a widespread phenomenon, Margaret Mead and the Samoans notwithstanding.[10]

RECENT STUDIES ON JEALOUSY.

Psychologists have recently discovered a number of important facts about jealousy.

People feel jealous because—

- *They feel left out or excluded;*
- *They feel insufficient time is spent with them;*
- *They feel loss of status or public esteem;*
- *They feel loss of power, control, or predictability with respect to the spouse.[11]*

Men and women differ in their feelings of jealousy:

- *Men become jealous when their spouse is sexually active with another man. This reflects on their own sexual adequacy. They also are jealous when they are compared with a rival male.*
- *Women become jealous when they experience a more generalized displacement by another woman and feel a lowering of self-esteem. They become jealous well before overt sexual intercourse occurs (1) when the spouse spends time with a competitor, (2) when the spouse talks to the competitor (by phone or in person), and (3) when the spouse kisses a female competitor.[12]*

The strategies for defense and coping are—

- *Indifference (frequent male response);*
- *Masochistic or martyr reaction (frequent female response);*
- *Defining the errant behavior as an affront to society rather than as a personal affront;*
- *Obsessive rumination and use of fantasy (What have I done wrong? What could I have done?);*

- *An attempt to sustain power or control over the spouse by threats or an appeal to duty or relentless supervision of spouse's activities;*

- *Sublimating the hurt through creative competition with the rival;*

- *Relabeling the jealousy as sexual arousal or pride in the partner;*

- *Constructive communication and discussion of the rules that govern the marriage.*[13]

IS JEALOUSY GOOD OR BAD? The question remains, Is jealousy good or bad? Psychologists stand on both sides of the question. In coping with it they suggest that jealousy be treated as a neutral phenomenon. They maintain that

> *if all jealousy is simply rejected as undesirable or immature, the effect goes underground and interferes with the couple's ability to deal with the feelings and communicate about the problem. If on the other hand it is praised, it may inhibit growth in the relationship. Jealousy, approached properly, offers an opportunity to discover new information about each other and the kind of relationships each desires.*[14]

POSSESSIVENESS AND JEALOUSY. Another approach is to distinguish between possessiveness and jealousy. Jealousy can be defined as a wholesome response to a real or perceived threat to a relationship, and possessiveness as an unwholesome, neurotic response to such a threat. The Bible speaks of God's jealousy over his chosen nation, Israel. Yet his jealousy did not interfere with Israel's determination to stray into idolatry or later reject God in the person of Jesus Christ. Jealousy values a relationship and pleads with the straying loved-one not to persist in the error of his way. But jealousy does not keep the loved-one captive. It loves that one enough to let him go.

In contrast with jealousy, possessiveness attempts to control the relationship against the will of the partner. Possessive people confuse their possessiveness with love. The husband who forbids his wife to use the telephone and car may say that he's doing it out of love. He may say he wants to protect her and the marriage against destructive forces from outside the home. But he is actually indulging his love for himself—a love that is threatened by his own insecurity and inadequacy. He won't face the fact that his feelings about his spouse are unjustified and that they are really a manifestation of his own neuroses. Instead, he attempts to control his wife to lessen his insecurity and inadequacy. In the process he destroys the relationship.

When Fran decided to leave Norman, her very possessive husband, she wrote him a letter to explain herself. She wrote him because he was too intimidating to talk to face-to-face.

After bidding him good-bye in her letter, she got down to explaining why she was leaving.

> I have been so dependent on you, so intimidated by your strength and self-assuredness for so long that I don't know any longer how to think or how I should feel about you and our marriage. Does that surprise you? I know you won't agree, but I am so emotionally dependent on you that I somehow misplaced part of myself. Every thought, every opinion, every feeling I have is a reaction to your thoughts, your opinions, and your feelings; sometimes the opposite because I feel defensive, sometimes the same because your feelings are so strong I'm afraid to disagree.

> I told you recently that I can't do special favors for you because you demand them before I have a chance to offer or make the gesture. Well, it's that way with my feelings too. I don't know how I feel until after I know how you feel.

Fran then expressed a desire for a reconciliation. But it never worked out because Norman never came to terms with his possessiveness.

The key difference between possessiveness and jealousy is that possessiveness attempts to control the other person. Jealousy states its case; possessiveness demands. Jealousy is the experience of an equal hurt by an equal; possessiveness is the experience of an owner outraged by the owned. Jealousy is willing to let the straying one go if it will help him see the error of his way. Possessiveness will not let go under any circumstances; it would rather see the other one destroyed than to let go.

COPING WITH JEALOUSY. Jealousy occurs in caring relationships. How do we cope with it? One woman says, "I feel so jealous when my husband talks about the camaraderie he shares with two of the women attorneys in his firm. They often lunch together and frequently work on cases together late at night and on weekends. My husband is very open about these friendships, and I know they are nothing more than that. But I still feel resentful. How can I get over these feelings?"[15]

This woman's counselor gave her some good advice. She needed to understand why she was jealous. Was it fear of losing her husband to a more desirable companion? It may be a realistic anxiety, and if so, she needed to talk with him about it, in a nonattacking manner. More often, jealousy arises from self-doubt. There's a fear of being rejected because we're not good enough. No matter how hard this woman tries, she'll never feel good enough, not because of a husband's conditional love, but because of her own self-doubt. People with good self-images tend not to be jealous, because they feel good about themselves and see no reason to be displaced by someone else.

A second kind of jealousy comes from feeling left out of the spouse's life. A wife's jealousy over her husband's friendships doesn't mean she should demand that he end them, particularly if they are true friendships—an appreciative-love rather than a need-love. She might occasionally join him and his female associates for lunch or include them in social gatherings at her home. Remember that two is not the necessary number for friendship.

Finally, jealousy may come from the feeling that her husband is giving the best of himself—his "quality" time and attention—to others. He has lunch with these women and works late with them. She feels that she seldom gets lunch or late-hour close contact with her husband. If this is how she feels, she must tell him by asking for an affirmation of his primary emotional commitment to her. Chances are, adjustments will be made to reinforce such a commitment. He will find ways to give his wife quality time and attention. But she must not be embarrassed to admit she's jealous. She can express it in a nonattacking, loving way as a problem that *she* is having. She may ask him to help her with her problem. How can he refuse?[16]

A man says, "My fiancee is still very friendly with her ex-husband. I can understand the need to communicate about the children, but I don't see why they have to be such good 'pals' with each other. They talk on the phone every time he calls to talk with the children. When he brings the children home, he often stays for dinner. Don't you think this relationship is peculiar?"[17]

It's not peculiar for ex-spouses to become friends after the conflicts of living together no longer exist. It's also in the best interests of the children that they work together as parents—as long as the children aren't given false hopes of reconciliation.

By airing these anxieties and resentments to her, this man puts his fiancee in a better position to make adjustments that will make him feel better. It's usually wise for ex-spouses to be businesslike, civil, and even friendly in their dealings with each other. Most good ex-spouse relationships reflect this quality. In coping with jealousy we must not be embarrassed to admit it, and we must communicate in a nonattacking, nondefensive, and loving manner.

WHAT ABOUT FORGIVENESS?

Joan was deeply troubled. When she came for counseling she said she had come for herself—she was the problem, not her husband, Nate.

She said that Nate had a friendship with a woman in his

office who, he later admitted, was more than just a friend. He had not been sexually unfaithful, but this woman had occupied his mind and emotions for a long time. He broke off his contacts with her, and subsequently she was transferred to another office. But this was not the problem.

Joan was troubled because she couldn't forgive Nate. "I'm angry and hurt that he did this to me. And the lies. He admits to them all. But I just can't forgive him."

THE BIBLICAL BASIS OF FORGIVENESS. Before helping Joan with her lack of forgiveness I had to be sure that there was a biblical basis for forgiveness to begin with. Did Nate acknowledge that he had sinned against his wife, had repented, and had asked her forgiveness? The Bible calls us to have a spirit of forgiveness, but the sinner has an obligation too: repentance. Jesus said, "If your brother sins, rebuke him, and if he repents, forgive him" (Luke 17:3).

Nate's attitude toward what he had done was all important. Sometimes when a wrong is done the wrongdoer will say, "I'm sorry you hurt." That's no apology! He needs to take responsibility for the hurt: "I'm sorry I hurt you."

Did Nate's behavior show that he grasped how deeply he had hurt Joan? Did he enter her world of pain with her by talking about it and letting her know that he felt her hurt?

This is what's required for forgiveness and fellowship in the church as stated in Matthew 18:15–18. Forgiveness and fellowship are not possible unless the offender acknowledges his guilt. If he does not hear you, your witnesses, or the church, "treat him as you would a pagan or a tax collector" (NIV). Emotional closeness is not possible without a credible acknowledgement of guilt. Distance from the offender is the only other choice.

DEALING WITH THE ANGER. Once we had a biblical basis for forgiveness we had to deal with Joan's anger. Joan was feeling guilty over her anger at Nate, but I had to show her that there was nothing wrong with it. Anger is a God-given emotion. The ability to be angry at wrongdoing shows we have been created in God's image. We don't always handle our anger properly, but anger itself is not wrong.

People from dysfunctional homes don't know how to deal constructively with anger because they have lived all their lives with one or the other of two destructive extremes. One is the family that represses anger and pretends that everything is fine. The other is the family that acts out anger destructively and abusively.

The Bible teaches a balance between these two extremes. In Ephesians 4:26 we are told that *we are to be angry* but not sin by repressing it and letting it develop into something worse.

It is true that Ephesians 4:31 tells us to get rid of all bitterness, rage, and anger. But we do it by expressing our anger before it becomes unmanageable.

I was able to help Joan get her anger out by encouraging her to express it and by teaching Nate how to express accurate empathy—how to enter her world of pain with her. Joan's healing didn't depend on her alone. It depended on a husband who was willing to do more than just say, "I'm sorry."

THIS KIND OF LOVE IS NOT ENOUGH

William Morris wrote a poem called "Love Is Enough" and someone reviewed it briefly in the words, "It isn't."[18] Natural love, which rises from our feelings, is not enough to sustain a marriage or repair a damaged one.

When a marriage is disrupted by physical or emotional infidelity, it's often assumed that there is a defect in the love relationship—love usually being understood as the feelings described in chapter 8, "an emotional high." But this kind of love is not enough. A different kind is required—"commitment."

Commitment is not usually thought of as love. It sounds too deliberate and unfeeling. Yet it is closely related to the most noble of all loves—*agape*—described in the New Testament as a love of choice or decision. We are told that when God sent his Son to die for our sins, he didn't do it because he felt emotionally attracted by our loveliness. We are reminded that while we were still sinners, he sent his Son to die for us (Rom. 5:8).

The love that rises out of choice or commitment is a high and holy love—an enduring love. It is not conditioned on the loveliness of the loved one. It is based on the commitment of the one who is giving love.

Commitment is properly called "gift-love." It differs from need-love in that the focus is not on what we get from it, but on what the other person gets. It gives a stability and durability to the relationship that need-love does not provide. As we have seen already, need-love lasts only as long as there is need. Once the need is satisfied or no longer exists, the loved-one is dismissed as being no longer necessary.

Though the institution of marriage was attacked in the turbulent sixties and seventies, it remains an institution because Americans are discovering that need-love is not enough. The commitment of marriage is all-important. A marriage license is not just a scrap of paper; it's a contract in which two people make a lifetime commitment to each other to "love, honor, and cherish, in sickness and in health, for better or for worse." Certain penalties are levied in divorce court for breach of this contract.

The commitment that is essential when a marriage is launched is just as important when the marriage is threatened by third-party interference. The only difference is that it seems easier to make a commitment to someone we're "in love with." This is not intended to belittle natural or romantic loves. One does not disparage a garden because it doesn't fence itself in, weed itself, or prune its own trees. A garden remains a garden as distinct from a wilderness only if someone tends it. It is that commitment to the garden that makes it teem with life and glow with color.

We don't deserve a great deal of credit for a garden's beauty. We are not creating something out of nothing. We are only tending it and permitting its natural beauty to blossom.

So it is with marriage. The labor of love seen in commitment makes it flourish. We do not create something from nothing. But we provide the conditions for it to show its unique beauty. And that labor must be done in love and not in the spirit of the prig or the Stoic.[19] We commit ourselves to our marriages believing that what we are committed to is big with splendor and vitality that we ourselves do not supply. Our responsibility is to liberate that splendor and let it be all that it can be.[20]

LEARNING TO TRUST AGAIN

A couple may give themselves to the task of cultivating their marriage garden, but they may expect to have some difficulty in learning to trust again—even if infidelity has been emotional rather than sexual.

This was the case with Jessie, mentioned earlier in this chapter. She felt a great deal of resentment over Walter's "friendship" with a young woman and had great difficulty trusting him and putting aside the fear of its happening again.

In counseling Jessie I shared my experience with a similar situation in my own marriage—a questionable friendship that I had had. My story proved to be helpful, because after Jessie returned home, she wrote my wife a lovely letter. It said in part,

> Dear Fay,
>
> Strange, how long it has been that I have yearned to talk with you. As Walter and I interacted with André through those difficult days I found myself thinking of you as being in the room with us. I would

think: what would Fay say to this, or would she understand how I am feeling just now? As those days stretched the closest I ever came to you was hearing André speak to you on the phone asking you to prepare coffee for us. I came to think of you as the "unseen presence" and influence in the room.

Of course all this was due to the fact that André was open enough with us to share in generalities your own struggles and we soon realized that his wisdom and help to us had come through the crucible of your own fires in your marriage. The outcome of your pain was comfort and hope for us. May I thank you for that? Thank you for fighting so hard for your own relationship that it made it possible for me to continue fighting. It made your husband effective. And it made me feel less alone. . . .

In reply Fay shared with Jessie her secret of learning to trust again.

Dear Jessie,

Thank you for your warm and friendly letter.

It always pleases me when I hear that Andy's and my experiences can be of help to others. The fact that Andy and I are able to conquer our problems through communication makes him a better counselor, I'm sure.

I'd like to share with you the way I was able to resolve my feelings of anger, hurt, and jealousy over a similar problem that you and Walter had recently concerning the young woman. I felt the one problem I would not be able to conquer was lack of trust. I didn't think I could ever totally trust Andy again. In talking with a counselor friend, I learned that no one can be totally trusted because we do not know from day to day what we will do or how we will respond in any given situation. What I can do is trust the commitment to the marriage that I know Andy has. I was then able to let go of the feelings of anxiety and suspicion, knowing that I would be able to deal with similar situations if they arose. I felt at peace knowing Andy is totally committed to our marriage and will not intentionally do anything to jeopardize it.

As to male-female friendships, I do not feel you are unreasonable in your feelings. As we do research for the friendship book we are coming more and more to the conclusion that male-female friendships are dangerous. The key issue is the meaning of the word "friendship." Is it appreciation or need? Are they shoulder to shoulder or face-to-face? We can answer this only by being totally honest with ourselves and each other. This requires the terribly painful process of talking it out—which you and Walter are doing.

Please do not lose heart while working on your marriage. If the commitment is there, then the problems can be conquered, and you will have a better marriage because of them and not in spite of them.

My prayers are with you.

To trust again is scary. It makes us vulnerable. But we really have no other choice. C. S. Lewis puts it this way:

To love at all is to be vulnerable. Love anything, and your heart will certainly be wrung and possibly be broken. If you want to make sure of keeping it intact, you must give your heart to no one, not even to an animal. Wrap it carefully round with hobbies and little luxuries; avoid all entanglements; lock it up safe in the casket or coffin of your selfishness. But in that casket—safe, dark, motionless, airless—it will change. It will not be broken; it will become unbreakable, impenetrable, irredeemable. The alternative to tragedy, or at least to the risk of tragedy, is damnation. The only place outside Heaven where you can be perfectly safe from all the danger and perturbations of love is Hell.[21]

NOTES

CHAPTER ONE: JUST FRIENDS

[1] Nancy Baker, "A Matter of Convenience," *Working Woman* (December 1982): 101.

[2] *Statistical Abstract of the United States: 1990* 110th edition (Washington: U.S. Bureau of Census, 1990): 386.

[3] C. S. Lewis, *The Four Loves* (New York: Harcourt Brace Jovanovich, 1960), 98–99.

CHAPTER TWO: WHAT IS FRIENDSHIP?

[1] Lewis, *The Four Loves*, 98.

[2] Ibid.

[3] Ibid., 96–97.

[4] Ibid., 91.

[5] Ibid., 104.

[6] Ibid., 92.

[7] Ibid., 102.

[8] Ibid., 95.

[9] Ibid., 31.

[10] Ibid., 32.

[11] Adler and Van Doren, *Great Treasury of Western Thought*, 242.

CHAPTER THREE: FRIENDSHIP AMERICAN STYLE

[1] *Family Therapy News* (July 1982): 8.

[2] *Psychology Today* (October 1979): 56.

[3] Ibid., 57, 59.

[4] Ibid., 59.

[5] Ibid., 57, 59.

[6] *Oxford English Dictionary,* 13 vols. (Oxford: At the Clarendon Press, 1961), 4:520.

[7] *Psychology Today* (June 1983): 25.

[8] *Essence* (October 1980): 118.

[9] Ibid.

[10] Ibid.

[11] *Mademoiselle* (April 1978): 203.

[12] Ibid.

[13] Ibid.
[14] *Mademoiselle* (May 1980): 142.
[15] *Mademoiselle* (April 1978): 142.

CHAPTER FOUR: THE FRIENDSHIP TEST

[1] *Webster's New World Dictionary*, 2d College Ed. (New York: World Publishing, 1970), 559, 738.
[2] *Mademoiselle* (May 1980): 142.
[3] Lewis, *The Four Loves*, 163.

CHAPTER FIVE: SUCCESSFUL OPPOSITE-SEX RELATIONSHIPS

[1] Julius Fast, *Body Language* (New York: Pocket Books, 1971), 1.
[2] *Psychology Today* (March 1979): 109.
[3] Fast, *Body Language*, 83.
[4] Ibid.
[5] *Family Therapy News* (July 1982): 10.
[6] *Focus on the Family* (June 1992): 2.
[7] Ibid.
[8] Ibid.
[9] Ibid.
[10] Fast, *Body Language*, 97.
[11] Eleanor Emmons Maccoby and Carol Nagy Jacklin, *The Psychology of Sex Differences* (Stanford, Calif.: Stanford University Press, 1974), vii.
[12] Ibid., 227–74.
[13] *Family Life Newspaper*, vol. 31, no. 2.
[14] Lewis, *The Four Loves*, 102–3.

CHAPTER SIX: ALTERNATIVES TO OPPOSITE-SEX FRIENDSHIPS

[1] Frank N. Magill, ed., *Masterplots*, vol. 5 (Englewood Cliffs, N.J.: Salem Press, 1976), 2854–55.
[2] Ralph Waldo Emerson, *Essays* (Chicago: Peoples Book Club, 1949), 130.
[3] Lewis, *The Four Loves*, 93–94.
[4] *Family Therapy News* (July 1982): 10.
[5] *Focus On the Family* (June 1992): 2.
[6] Ibid.
[7] Ibid.
[8] *Glamour* (April 1979): 152.
[9] Ibid.
[10] *Mademoiselle* (April 1978): 212.
[11] Ibid.
[12] Ibid., 212–13.
[13] Ibid., 213.

CHAPTER SEVEN: SINGLES' FRIENDSHIPS

[1] *Solo* (Spring 1983): 11.
[2] Lewis, *The Four Loves*, 102.
[3] *Solo* (Spring 1983): 42
[4] Carolyn Koons, *Tony: Our Journey Together* (New York: Harper & Row, 1984).

CHAPTER EIGHT: MAKING YOUR MATE YOUR BEST FRIEND

[1] *Family Therapy News* (July 1982): 10.
[2] Everett Shostrom, *Caring Relationship Inventory Manual* (San Diego: Educational and Industrial Testing Service, 1966), 4–5.
[3] Sheri S. Tepper, *So Your Happily Ever After Isn't* (Denver: RMPP Publications, 1977), 2.
[4] Ibid., 3.

CHAPTER NINE: WHEN THERE'S SOMEONE ELSE

[1] *Time* (January 13, 1983): 80.
[2] *Redbook* (July 1976): 163.
[3] *Time* (January 13, 1983): 80.
[4] John D. Davis, ed., *The Westminster Dictionary of the Bible* (Philadelphia: Westminster Press, 1944), 111.
[5] Walter Trobisch, *My Wife Made Me a Polygamist* (Downers Grove, Ill.: InterVarsity Press, 1971), 18–19.
[6] *Good Housekeeping* (May 1978): 202.
[7] Ibid.
[8] Ibid., 203.
[9] Janice L. Francis, "Toward Management of Heterosexual Jealousy," *Journal of Marriage and Family Counseling*, vol. 3, no. 4 (October 1977): 64.
[10] *Time* (February 14, 1983): 68–69.
[11] Francis, "Toward Management of Heterosexual Jealousy," 64.
[12] Ibid.
[13] Ibid., 65.
[14] Ibid.
[15] *McCall's* (March 1980): 90.
[16] Ibid.
[17] Ibid.
[18] Lewis, *The Four Loves*, 163.
[19] Ibid., 165.
[20] Ibid.
[21] Ibid., 169.

INDEX